THE PAST IN PERSPECTIVE

NAPOLEON COMES TO POWER

DEMOCRACY AND DICTATORSHIP IN REVOLUTIONARY FRANCE, 1795–1804

Malcolm Crook

© Malcolm Crook, 1998

British Library Cataloguing-In-Publication Data.
A catalogue record for this book is available from the British
Library.

ISBN (paperback) 0-7083-1401-5
      (cased) 0-7083-1461-9

The right of Malcolm Crook to be identified as author of this work
has been asserted by him in accordance with the Copyright, Designs
and Patents Act 1988.

Typeset at the University of Wales Press
Printed in Great Britain by Dinefwr Press, Llandybïe

In memory of

GUY AMUSAN

(1942–1992)

Frequently late in this world, tragically early for the next

Contents

Editors' Foreword

Each volume in this series, *The Past in Perspective*, deals with a major theme of British, European or World history. The aim of the series is to engage the interest of all for whom knowledge of the riches of the world's historical experience is a delight, and in particular to meet the needs of students of history in universities and colleges — and at comparatively modest cost.

Each theme is tackled at sufficient length and in sufficient depth to allow each writer both to advance our understanding of the subject in the light of the most recent research, and to place his or her approach in due perspective. Accordingly, each volume contains a historiographical chapter which assesses how interpretations of its theme have developed, and have been criticized, endorsed, modified or discarded. Each volume, too, includes a section of substantial excerpts from key original sources: this reflects the importance of allowing the reader to come to his or her own conclusions about differing interpretations, and also the greater accessibility nowadays of original sources in print. Furthermore, in each volume there is a detailed bibliography which not only underpins the writer's own account and analysis, but also enables the reader to pursue the theme, or particular aspects of it, to even greater depth; the explosion of historical writing in the twentieth century makes such guidance invaluable. By these perspectives, taken together, each volume is an up-to-date, authoritative and substantial exploration of themes, ancient, medieval or modern, of British, European, American or World significance, after more than a century of the study and teaching of history.

C. C. Eldridge and Ralph A. Griffiths

Explanatory note
Reference to the Illustrative Documents which follow the main text

are indicated by a bold roman numeral preceded by the word 'DOCUMENT', all within square brackets [**DOCUMENT XII**].

Acknowledgements

It was Ralph Griffiths, one of the editors for this series, who invited me to write this study and then offered helpful advice during its gestation. I owe Ralph a great debt, for he encouraged me enormously during the halcyon days I spent as an undergraduate at Swansea and he has continued to take an interest in my progress ever since. A number of specialists in this period of French history have also supplied invaluable advice and assistance, including Steven Clay and Edward A. Arnold and, above all, my good friend John Dunne. Finally, I should like to thank the staff at the University of Wales Press for their unfailing cheerfulness and patience with a rather tardy author: our acquaintance has been a most enjoyable one.

Malcolm Crook
Keele University, January 1998

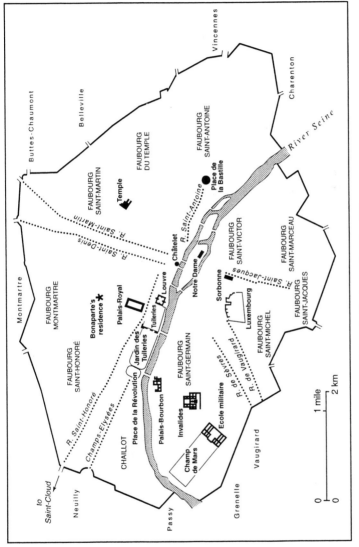

Map 1: Paris under the Directory.

Map 2: The Departments of the French Republic in 1799.

1. Triumph or Tragedy? The Debate on Napoleon's Seizure of Power

Napoleon Bonaparte, the Revolution's most famous general, came to power in November 1799, during the eighth year of the First French Republic. It was the month of Brumaire according to the revolutionary calendar then in use, the name suggesting a period of fog and mist, a suitably murky context for the conspiracy in which Napoleon and a syndicate of leading republicans were involved. They considered that major revisions to the political system were necessary, to provide more vigorous executive authority at a time when revolutionary France was once again deep in crisis, buckling under renewed pressure from both inside and outside the country. Change could not be achieved within the current constitution, so the veteran politician Sieyès and his allies recruited General Bonaparte to help them impose emergency measures and create a new regime in which they would play a dominant role.

The famous *coup d'état* of Brumaire Year VIII has become the archetype of movements that overthrow governments 'from above', as opposed to the popular insurrection that subverts authority 'from below', though contemporaries referred to this event as a revolution and not as a *coup*. It took two days to effect, beginning in the early hours of 18 Brumaire (9 November 1799). Carefully selected members of the Council of Elders (one of two existing legislative bodies) were summoned by officials to meet at the Tuileries later that morning, in order to consider transferring the location of their sessions outside Paris (see map of Paris on p.xi). The officials were party to Sieyès's plot, and other conspirators were soon at work persuading the Elders that a popular uprising to overthrow the Republic was about to erupt in the capital. The Elders readily agreed to leave Paris for the outskirts of the city, where they would reconvene next day at the Château of Saint-Cloud. There, removed from public scrutiny, it was hoped that deputies would consent more readily to the establishment of a more powerful executive body.

General Bonaparte, who represented the military arm of the conspiracy, was entrusted with arranging security measures to facilitate the transfer and with safeguarding the nation's representatives in the process. He made his way to the Council of Elders, to be sworn in as commander-in-chief of the troops, though significantly he made no reference to upholding the Constitution in the oath he took. As befitted the hero of epic campaigns in Italy and Egypt, he received rapturous applause from the waiting soldiery when he re-emerged from the chamber later on the morning of 18 Brumaire and promised to revive the flagging fortunes of France. The resolution to move the assemblies was subsequently submitted to the Council of Five Hundred, the other legislative body, which was meeting on the opposite bank of the River Seine. Some objections to the transfer were raised but, according to the text of the existing Constitution, it was the Elders who decided where the two Councils sat and any concerted resistance would have been illegal.

The five-man executive Directory (which gave its name to the French republican regime that was established in the wake of the Terror and lasted from 1795 to 1799) had effectively been bypassed by this parliamentary manœuvre; now it was disbanded. Two of its members, Sieyès and the self-effacing Ducos, were among the conspirators who had instigated the coup and they immediately resigned their offices. A third Director, the long-serving but discredited Barras, was cajoled into quitting by a combination of bribery and his realization that opposition would be futile. The two remaining Directors, Gohier and Moulin, stubbornly refused to follow suit, but they were simply confined to their residence at the Luxembourg Palace and placed under armed guard. The government of France had effectively ceased to exist.

The night of 18–19 Brumaire (9–10 November) passed in calm; the alleged uprising on the streets of Paris was, of course, a fabrication and the capital had not stirred. So far events had unfolded smoothly; the outcome of the following day, 19 Brumaire, remained uncertain, however. Protests were anticipated, especially from Jacobin radicals in the Council of Five Hundred which, like the Council of Elders, was not scheduled to meet at Saint-Cloud until midday. The conspirators were taking a deliberate risk in prolonging the *coup* in order to preserve a semblance of legality. All being well, once they had been informed of the resignation of the Directors, the two legislative bodies were expected to nominate a provisional government to replace them and thus put the conspirators into power. In the event, the deputies proceeded in a rather dilatory fashion and Bonaparte grew nervous and impatient; indeed, he provoked an outcry when, early on the afternoon of 10 November, he marched in to address the Council of Elders and then the Five Hundred. In the former his appearance attracted hostile comment, while in the latter he was manhandled by angry deputies, and two lofty grenadiers were obliged to help him withdraw.

The game was up. In the Council of Five Hundred it was suggested that a motion be put to declare General Bonaparte an outlaw and relieve him of his command. Napoleon's brother, Lucien, who was chairman of the Five Hundred, sought to end the uproar, but the best he could do was effectively to suspend the session by vacating his place and rejoining the general outside. There was no alternative now but to use the troops, who were enraged by reports that Bonaparte's life had been threatened, to clear the hall where the Five Hundred were sitting. Confronted with bayonets, the deputies scattered, but all hope of the conspiracy succeeding via a legitimate parliamentary manœuvre was lost as a result.

In a desperate effort to preserve a façade of legality, the conspirators hastily rounded up a rump assembly of deputies, many of whom had taken refuge in the gardens of the chateau. These somewhat reluctant collaborators were then persuaded to appoint a temporary executive of three consuls, comprising Sieyès, Ducos and Bonaparte in that order. They also agreed to adjourn the legislative bodies, so that two commissions could revise the Constitution, and to sanction the arrest of some sixty determined opponents of the conspiracy. A sanitized version of events was subsequently produced and widely circulated. Yet news of the *coup* excited little reaction in Paris and produced few hostile responses from the provinces.

The three provisional consuls proceeded to install themselves in the Luxembourg Palace, in place of the five Directors, suggesting business as usual and few dramatic changes. Indeed, at the first meeting of the Provisional Consulate, it was decided to rotate the chairmanship; Bonaparte initially presided, but only by virtue of alphabetical precedence over Ducos and Sieyès. It was Napoleon's subsequent insistence that he should become all-powerful First Consul under the new constitution, which revealed the real significance of Brumaire; some historians have described the manipulation of the political settlement in Napoleon's favour as a further *coup d'état*. The general had clearly emerged victorious over his fellow conspirators. The experiment with a liberal republic had come to an end and the Bonapartist dictatorship was about to begin. How had it happened?

The Napoleonic legend

Bonaparte was always his own best apologist, not least in the statements he made during the final years of his life, which he spent confined on the island fastness of St Helena in the South Atlantic. *The Memorial of St Helena*, based on a series of conversations with Las Cases, a French aristocrat who accompanied him into exile after 1815, played a crucial role in fostering his legend. The *Memorial* has been aptly described as one of the most important texts for understanding the history of nineteenth-century France, yet it has little to say about how Napoleon came to power, save for a typically pragmatic justification of the *coup*:

> People are still engaged in abstract discussion as to whether our action on 18 Brumaire was a legal or a criminal one. At best, however, these are theories suitable for books or public oratory, which lose their significance when applied to the real world. It is like condemning a sailor for chopping off a mast to escape a shipwreck. The perpetrators of this revolution could reply to their accusers as did the Romans of old: 'Our act is justified in that we saved the Republic; let us therefore render thanks to the gods.'

The highly selective, Bonapartist version of the events of Brumaire was in fact formulated immediately after the *coup d'état* took place. Though Bonaparte was but one member of a three-man Consulate, there was no sign of fellow conspirators in the first proclamation that was rushed off the presses in the early hours of 20 Brumaire (11 November 1799) and circulated throughout the country:

> On my return to Paris [in 1799], I found division among all the authorities and agreement upon only one point, namely, that the Constitution was half-destroyed and unable to save liberty. All parties came to see me, and confided their plans to me, revealed their secrets, and requested my support; I refused to be the man of any party.

Napoleon's claim to have spurned the factions, in order to raise himself above the sordid political arena, struck a powerful chord, allowing him to conclude this key document with the ringing words:

> Frenchmen, without doubt you will recognize in this conduct all
> the zeal of a soldier of liberty, a citizen devoted to the Republic.
> Conservative, tutelary and liberal ideas have been restored to their
> rightful place by the dispersal of the agitators who oppressed the
> Councils and who, having become the most odious of men, have not
> ceased to be the most contemptible. [**DOCUMENT I**]

The idea of the saviour rescuing France from chaos constituted the
basic explanation for the rise of Napoleon in all subsequent
sympathetic accounts. Armand Lefebvre's *History of the Cabinets of
Europe during the Consulate and the Empire*, for instance, was primarily
a study of international relations, written by a career diplomat and
published during the late 1840s. Yet it was set in the domestic context
of Napoleonic France and began with a defence of the *coup* of
Brumaire. According to Lefebvre, ten years of upheaval had left the
country in a state of perpetual crisis. In 1799, racked by confusion
and dissent, the Republic was on the point of exhaustion; the other
European powers, relishing the spectacle of internal dissolution, were
like vultures eagerly awaiting the opportunity to devour their prey.
The overthrow of the ineffectual executive Directory was, therefore,
absolutely essential; the urgent need for Napoleon to act far
outweighed any injustice or impropriety in the way his remedial
action was conducted. The end justified the means.

This constant refrain in Bonapartist historiography is best
exemplified by Albert Vandal's classic, though untranslated
L'Avènement de Bonaparte (The Advent of Napoleon), which
appeared in two volumes at the turn of the twentieth century, a
hundred years after the event. This eloquent account made no
attempt to hide its author's pronounced admiration for Napoleon. It
naturally commenced with a justification of the *coup d'état*:

> The men who took control of the Revolution after the 9 Thermidor
> [the overthrow of Robespierre and the end of the Terror] remained a
> faction, incapable of becoming a legitimate government. They resorted
> to illegality to remain in office, but without consolidating their
> position, and a series of crises explains why the more intelligent among
> them eventually decided to seek, instead of the existing regime, a
> powerful individual who could guarantee their interests and restore
> order.

Vandal defended Napoleon from the charge of destroying liberty by arguing that by the time that the general returned to France from his famous Egyptian campaign, in the autumn of 1799, the French people had long been deprived of freedom; 'Bonaparte could not suppress something that did not exist', he concluded. **[DOCUMENT II]**
On the contrary, the general successfully endeavoured to restore stability and harmony in place of the anarchy and division that a decade of revolution had inflicted on France. He sought to pacify rather than to proscribe. By avoiding the extremes of left and right, settling the religious issue and even securing a (brief) European peace, the Consulate which Napoleon headed from 1799 to 1804 marked a resounding triumph, creating many enduring features of modern France in the process. For many years after the Revolution, republicanism was equated with anarchy and civil war, so the glory and stability of the Napoleonic era offered a potent vision. Vandal's latter-day imitators, however, who remain alive and well at the Institut Napoléon in Paris, have never matched his eloquence. In any case, Bonapartism lost much of its attraction with the establishment of a viable republican system in France in the twentieth century.

The republican tradition

The republican critique of Napoleon's rise to power in the wake of the French Revolution only began to crystallize in the middle of the nineteenth century, in opposition to the Second Empire founded by Louis Napoleon, a nephew of the great Bonaparte. Yet one contemporary critic of the *coup d'état* deserves a mention under this heading. Madame de Staël, daughter of the *ancien-régime* finance minister Necker, was a liberal intellectual whose brave and outspoken hostility to the Napoleonic dictatorship was rewarded with exile to her native Switzerland. Her critical comments on Brumaire, which appeared in the historical analysis, *Considerations on the French Revolution*, were only published after her death, in 1818.
According to de Staël, the military crisis brought about by the Second European Coalition against France had been resolved by the time Bonaparte came to power. 'It was not, therefore, external reverses that produced the fatal attraction to Bonaparte in 1799, but rather the fear inspired by the Jacobins inside the country which worked so powerfully in his favour', she wrote. Even the Jacobins no

longer represented any real threat, so the nation surrendered simply in order 'to escape from a phantom'. Thus the country was conquered by one of its own generals, through the complaisance of an army anxious to see one of its leaders in charge. True, France at the end of the revolutionary decade was no great model of a constitutional state, but it retained the potential to learn from its mistakes. After Brumaire this possibility disappeared as Bonaparte ushered in an iron age of despotism, which suppressed freedom and stifled artistic life. [**DOCUMENT III**]

Later republican writers magnified this mirror image of the Bonapartist legend, depicting Napoleon as an assassin of liberty rather than as the saviour of France. A second short-lived Republic, founded in 1848, was overthrown by another Bonapartist *coup* in 1851, when Louis Napoleon came to power and created a Second Empire. This apparent repetition of Brumaire naturally served to stimulate fresh reflections upon the demise of democracy at the end of the eighteenth century. It also added urgency to the quest for an alternative reading of French history, to demonstrate that liberal democracy had enjoyed a successful apprenticeship until it was cynically curtailed by an earlier dictator.

Thus Edgar Quinet, a higher-education lecturer exiled from France after the downfall of the Second Republic, led the assault in 1865, with an analysis of the revolutionary decade which encompassed the Consulate and was simply entitled *The Revolution*. Echoing de Staël, he denounced the events of 18 Brumaire: 'As long as there was a civilian government, and a constitution, and a republic, there were at least the roots from which liberty might still spring, to blossom once more; now there came, with the sword, a regime on principle opposed to liberty.' Quinet emphasized the violence which accompanied the second day of the *coup*, deliberately omitted from the Bonapartist account in order to create an aura of legality. No wonder it was always 18 Brumaire, when in fact the decisive day of the *coup*, 19 Brumaire, 'added force to the trickery of the previous day', as the outcome was decided by swords and bayonets. Such a military solution to the political problems of the Republic could only lead in the direction of despotism and slavery.

The republican journalist Pierre Lanfrey continued the onslaught when his *History of Napoleon* began to appear a couple of years later. Ostensibly an impartial account, scientifically based on newly available documentation, this was a polemic, intended to sap the foundations of the Second Empire as much as to undermine the reputation of the first Napoleon. Lanfrey's Bonaparte was driven solely by personal ambition and, far from consolidating the Revolution, he destroyed it, via a *coup* that was presented to the public through a tissue of lies. 'History has recorded many a solemn falsehood', he wrote, 'but it would be difficult to cite one in which truth has been outraged with more cynicism and shamelessness . . . Such was the début of the new government, and such was the man for whom the public liberties had been sacrificed.' What Napoleon created instead was a regime that suppressed freedom of speech, the press and parliament; it possessed few redeeming features.

By the time Lanfrey's final volume appeared, in the 1870s, the Second Empire had fallen, to be supplanted by the Third Republic, which was to prove much more enduring than its short-lived predecessors. The first centenary of the Revolution in 1889 served to consecrate this long-awaited republican triumph and, besides the erection of the Eiffel tower in Paris, it brought the creation of the Chair of the French Revolution at the Sorbonne (University of Paris). Alphonse Aulard, the first occupant of this prestigious post, subtitled his great *Political History of the French Revolution* 'The Origins and Development of Democracy in France', and he concluded his history in 1804 at the creation of the First Empire. When Bonaparte placed a crown upon his head, 'imperial despotism definitively ended the Revolution and marked a temporary reversion to the *ancien régime* by abolishing liberty and renouncing equality'.

While it was relatively easy to condemn Bonaparte's *coup* and its authoritarian outcome, republican historians found it much harder to defend the apparently ramshackle directorial regime that preceded it. Aulard attempted to rebut the argument in favour of Napoleon's intervention by pointing to the achievements of the Directory and by emphasizing external factors in its demise. He began his chapter on the downfall of the Directory with the comment: 'The *coup d'état* of 18 Brumaire, by means of which Bonaparte confiscated the Republic and ended the Revolution, was ultimately and indirectly, yet none the less clearly, the result of the 20 April 1792, when the Legislative Assembly declared war on the Habsburg Monarchy.' Thereafter France was continually at war since, in spite of many great victories, peace could not be obtained. This armed struggle served to stunt the country's constitutional growth because liberty was constantly violated. In order to prosecute the war effectively, a strong executive was required, yet, once established, it all too frequently overrode the sovereignty of the people. The way was thus prepared for an ambitious general to render himself supreme.

Aulard blamed the outside circumstances of the war for the unconstitutional behaviour of the Directory (as well as highlighting the unreasonableness of the royalists), but he also identified a 'degeneration of patriotism' into militarism. The army became a force in its own right, the only vigorous institution in the state, and the politicians compounded the problem by using the army to resolve internal affairs, chiefly in order to save their own political skins. The army began to entertain political aspirations; after all, it had organized the land it conquered when the war began to prove successful in the late 1790s. The army loved the Republic, but not civil liberty, and began to feel that it should take charge of domestic affairs too.

After his victories in Italy, Bonaparte became the darling of public opinion, and on his return to France from Egypt (a campaign which had increased his popularity, despite its lack of success), he began to conspire with Sieyès to overthrow the Directory. Yet, argued Aulard, even then the nation had no desire for a *coup d'état*. The frontiers were safe, royalist insurrection was under control and the legislature was in the process of repealing the draconian measures passed in the depths of the crisis of the summer of 1799; the conspirators had to act quickly to preserve a pretext for their action. The 18 Brumaire was thus fraudulently founded and public opinion was cynically manipulated to acquiesce in a gradual erosion of liberty.

The Marxist interpretation

Karl Marx himself made few references to Napoleon Bonaparte in his voluminous outpourings, beyond suggesting that he exploited the revolutionary heritage for his own ends, replacing permanent upheaval with permanent warfare. However, Marx did write a great deal about his own mid-nineteenth-century contemporary, Bonaparte's nephew, the Emperor Napoleon III. In *The Eighteenth Brumaire of Louis Napoleon*, which sought to explain Napoleon III's rise to power in 1851, Marx began with the memorable phrase: 'History repeats itself, the first time as tragedy, the second time as farce', and he also commented that 'men make their own history, but not in circumstances of their own choosing'. It is possible to derive some perspectives on the first Napoleon from this analysis. Marxist historians have accordingly been anxious to locate Bonaparte's advent to power squarely in the context of a decade of revolution. They have stressed the combination of economic and social factors obtaining at the turn of the nineteenth century that facilitated, even necessitated, the establishment of his dictatorship.

The Marxist interpretation, which dominated the history of the French Revolution for much of the twentieth century, did not focus on the Napoleonic period in particular, but always sought to set the regime within the wider framework of 'the bourgeois revolution of 1789'. In the process, historians influenced by Marx naturally tended to reduce the importance of the Brumaire *coup* which, in their view, merely consolidated the ascendancy of the bourgeoisie, albeit at the cost of sacrificing political liberty. Georges Lefebvre, who succeeded to the Chair of the French Revolution at the Sorbonne just before the Second World War, wrote in his conclusion to *The Directory*: 'This is the real significance of the 18 Brumaire: initiated by a few bold bourgeois, it decisively entrenched the power of the bourgeoisie.'

In his two-volume history entitled *Napoleon*, he struck a deterministic note, which further diminished the individual stature of Bonaparte:

> That the French Revolution turned to dictatorship was no accident; it was driven there by inner necessity, and not for the first time either. Nor was it an accident that the Revolution led to the dictatorship of a general, but it so happened that this general was Napoleon Bonaparte. **[DOCUMENT IV]**

Albert Soboul, who later occupied the same Chair of the Revolution in the 1970s, followed closely in Lefebvre's intellectual footsteps:

> After Fructidor and Campoformio [key events in 1797, inside and outside France, which temporarily bolstered the republican regime], the Directory's policies were marked by increasing recourse to authoritarian methods. The government gained thereby a certain effectiveness and was able to implement important administrative reforms which paved the way for those of the Consulate. With the regime's social foundation still narrowly defined, however, political stabilization proved impossible. The system managed to survive, so long as continental peace lasted - although even then only at the price of more attacks on the liberal workings of the Constitution of Year III. The formation of the Second Coalition and the resumption of the war

in 1799 precipitated the final crisis. The *coup d'état* of 18 Brumaire reconciled the restoration of state authority with the social predominance of the fraction of the bourgeoisie who were notables. Yet because the notables had been obliged to avail themselves of the help of the army in this journée, they thereby lost their political power.

Soboul explicitly linked Bonaparte to the Revolution in a little book that treated Directory and Consulate as a single entity. The real end to the Revolution, for him as for so many other historians, came with the creation of the First French Empire in 1804, when Bonaparte cut himself off from the revolutionary heritage and created a popular monarchy, a political hybrid of limited duration.

Current perspectives

The overarching approach characteristic of the Marxist interpretation has the great merit of situating the *coup d'état* of Brumaire firmly in its wider historical context and provides a framework within which recent research has been conducted. Indeed, echoes of the Marxian tradition remain and inform Martyn Lyons's excellent, recent study *Napoleon Bonaparte and the Legacy of the French Revolution*. In his introduction, Lyons states that 'Napoleon will be discussed as part of the Revolution, preserving its social gains and consecrating the triumph of the bourgeoisie':

> Brumaire then, did not announce the end of the principles of the French Revolution. It signified rather that one particular institutional form of those revolutionary ideals had served out its usefulness, and succumbed to history. The revolutionary bourgeois of France . . . needed to defend their gains . . . the Directory no longer provided a sufficient guarantee; they turned to a new set of institutions to protect the legacy of the French Revolution. The *coup* of Brumaire may best be interpreted not as a rupture with the immediate revolutionary past, but as a new attempt to secure and prolong the hegemony of the revolutionary bourgeoisie. It was ironic that the French bourgeoisie, usually so timid, concerned with stability and wary of risk, had entrusted the Revolution to a diminutive Corsican soldier . . . [**DOCUMENT V**]

In France in the 1970s, under the influence of the so-called *Annales* school which flourished around the journal of that name, historians were encouraged to explore long-term developments rather than short-term political events or outstanding personalities. Bonaparte was almost written out of the historical script as a result. Louis Bergeron's brilliant study, translated as *France under Napoleon*, is more literally rendered into English as *The Napoleonic Episode*. The original title deliberately conveyed the transience of the man and the political arrangements he engineered, in order to stress the more enduring and only slowly evolving 'structures' that underpinned his regime. Much of the book is addressed to those developments that eluded Napoleon's grasp – population growth and social change, for example. Bergeron begins his book by stating: 'As for 18 Brumaire and the Constitution of the Year VIII (1799), we need not assign a special importance . . . to the political event itself . . .' Yet, even Bergeron concedes that, 'the *coup d'état* of General Bonaparte was unlike those that preceded it . . . His rule was to mark the end of the Revolution, a return to order and stability . . .'

The emphasis on social and economic factors is no longer so fashionable in writing about the past, but other historians have picked up Bergeron's reference to the significance of Brumaire. François Furet, one of the so-called 'revisionist' historians who has called into question many aspects of the classic Marxist interpretation, prefers to underline the failure of the Revolution to entrench a liberal, pluralistic political culture in France. Thus, Napoleon was 'chosen by the Revolution, from which he received his strange power not only to embody the new nation . . . but also to fulfil its destiny'. As for the *coup*: 'Well-conceived but executed in panic, 18 Brumaire enjoyed the nation's blessing before the fact.' This was a dictatorship of public opinion, intended to consolidate the Revolution, to end the revolutionary romance and mark the beginning of its real history. Aspirations were finally translated into concrete achievements, combining the results of a decade of experiment with the traditions of a strong state bequeathed by the French monarchy.

Furet's approach has been criticized for replacing the social and economic determinism of the Marxists with an ideological determinism that highlights the weakness of liberalism in France and condemns the Revolution to an authoritarian outcome under Bonaparte. By contrast, the reaction against an impersonal, scientific and 'structural' history has reawakened interest in the historical role of outstanding individuals. In the case of Napoleon, about whom so much has already been written, the risk of biographical repetition and hero worship is considerable. There remains an apparently insatiable thirst for the details of Napoleon's personal life – his relationship with Josephine, or the cause of his death on St Helena, for instance – what the French call *la petite histoire*. It is, however, possible to present a more open-ended account of the events of Brumaire, acknowledging the influence of particular personalities, whilst avoiding the pitfalls of both hagiography and historical trivia.

Jean Tulard, the current doyen of Napoleonic studies in France, called his major work of synthesis, *Napoleon: The Myth of the Saviour*. As the title suggests, this is by no means an uncritical work, but it stresses the ways in which Napoleon personally incarnated much of the development of France, both past and present. Tulard also attributes a greater role to Bonaparte himself, by suggesting that the nature of his regime was determined by the choice he made in 1799 between a renewed Jacobin dictatorship, the consolidation of the Directory and the *coup* proposed by Sieyès. The last of these alternatives was adopted, yet Brumaire was more than just another in a series of *coups d'état*, for, as the more prescient politicians realized, Bonaparte was determined to turn it to his own advantage. For Tulard, Brumaire did not represent another phase of revolution, but rather the end of the Revolution, an objective that politicians had been pursuing in France since 1791.

Ending a revolution is no easy task, yet it is a subject that has scarcely attracted the attention of historians and political scientists, who have been far more preoccupied with explaining how revolutions begin. Yet to destroy is far easier than to build, especially upon the shaky foundations of liberty, equality and fraternity. The termination of the French Revolution under Napoleon will be a major theme of the chapters that follow. The Directory had set itself the same demanding objective when it was created in 1795, so why did it fail and give Bonaparte his opportunity four years later? This question is the subject of the next chapter, for of late the neglected and much-maligned directorial regime has been treated more sympathetically by historians.

In the past Napoleon has been seen as conducting an act of merciful euthanasia upon a moribund body politic. Martyn Lyons has suggested that 'if Bonaparte was the gravedigger of political liberty, the Directory had already presented him with the corpse'. Recent research into the Directory, much of it inspired by conferences organized in France to mark the two-hundredth anniversary of this period, suggests that the political impasse was not as insoluble as Bonapartist apologists would have us believe. The

Directory had a number of innovations to its credit and it can be argued that there were viable, liberal alternatives available in 1799. Despite the difficult situation that prevailed in the wake of the Terror, the Directory had achievements to its credit and many of them paved the way for Napoleon's later successes.

The events of Brumaire can only be treated in detail and properly evaluated against this background. The contingent nature of the *coup* also needs stressing, since it very nearly came to grief. The third chapter will closely examine the origins and formation of the conspiracy led by Sieyès and Napoleon, before following the way it unfolded, and nearly unravelled, on 18 and 19 Brumaire. The overthrow of the Directory was certainly not greeted with any great enthusiasm. Its presentation to the public was, therefore, a vital aspect of its ultimate success. The way in which the advent of the new regime was conveyed to the public represented a great stroke of propaganda which will be considered in some detail. Attitudes and opinions were moulded to accept the *coup* as a great turning point, the meaning of which was the foundation of a post-revolutionary order in France.

Even so, the establishment of the Napoleonic regime was far from being a foregone conclusion, and this remained the case long after the Provisional Consulate had been set up on the 19 Brumaire. As always, to entrench a regime proved far more difficult than seizing power in the first place. Napoleon was not the first to declare that the Revolution was over and there was no guarantee that he would be the last. The politicians who backed Brumaire were a diverse group, whose unity began to fracture as soon as their joint efforts to overturn the Directory succeeded. Many of them were dismayed by the supremacy that Bonaparte achieved, and actively opposed his authoritarianism in the legislative organs retained by the Constitution of the Year VIII. On the other hand, the army was dismayed by some of Bonaparte's conciliatory gestures towards counter-revolutionaries, though royalist hopes were dashed as rapidly as they had been raised.

Too little is known about the consolidation of the Bonapartist regime, which will be treated in a fourth and final chapter. Biographies and military histories abound, but academic interest in the politics of the Napoleonic period remains slight, even in France. On the whole, historians have been much more anxious to study the upheaval of the 1790s than to examine a return to order, which brought the dead hand of conformity and bureaucracy in its wake. It must be hoped that the rapidly approaching bicentenary of Napoleon's advent to power in the *coup d'état* of Brumaire will, like the two-hundredth anniversary of his birth in 1969, stimulate some serious work on this period rather than simply encourage the recycling of existing material.

Enough research has already been done, however, at both national and local level, to revise the conclusions of many of the older, general histories, though the great bulk of recent work remains inaccessible to English readers. It suggests that the First Consul did gradually succeed in winning popular support, by means of repression as well as reconciliation. He was able to rally personnel from the old regime and the new and to put them into administrative harness together. Tradition and innovation were blended into an effective synthesis that was both authoritarian and egalitarian. His growing popularity was reflected in the referendum on the Life Consulate in 1802, which, unlike the consultation following his seizure of power at the end of 1799, did genuinely attract a massive turnout.

Subsequent changes, above all the foundation of the Empire in 1804, the chronological point at which this book ends, were to prove less enduring. There was a fundamental contradiction in the efforts of a self-made leader to create a hereditary dynasty and, when Napoleon fell a decade later, his regime collapsed with him. The French were to experience a long struggle in their quest for political stability and a constitutional framework to fit the social and cultural changes registered by the Revolution. Yet by establishing a solid administrative and legal system, Bonaparte can be said to have halted the forward march of the revolutionary process. Though this was not obvious at the time, there is no doubt that the *coup d'état* of Brumaire marked a watershed in the course of French history.

2. The Impossible Republic? The Road to Brumaire, 1795–1799

The Directory, the liberal republican regime that ruled France after 1795, has been the object of unrelenting criticism. Rarely considered worthy of serious attention, it has received short shrift – sometimes none at all – from historians anxious to hail Bonaparte as the mighty conquering hero who overcame the corrupt, ineffectual politicians and restored French greatness in Europe. The years 1795 to 1799 are usually seen either as an anodyne aftermath of the Terror, or as the lack-lustre prelude to Napoleon. The period is seldom viewed on its own terms as a significant attempt to combine liberty and equality within a republican framework which, with the benefit of hindsight, might be regarded as the historic goal of the French Revolution. It is frequently forgotten that the Directory lasted longer than any preceding revolutionary regime, while the Constitution of 1795 on which it was based proved more enduring than the brief constitutions of Bonaparte's Consulate that immediately followed.

Clearly the context in which Napoleon came to power is crucial to an understanding of how and why he did so, not to mention the problems he would encounter afterwards. Had the Constitution of 1795 provided a satisfactory basis for ending the Revolution by restoring stability, then there would have been no need for dictatorship. Of course, it is easy to exaggerate the shortcomings of the Directory, after the manner of Bonapartist apologists, in order to map out a clear path to Brumaire. Recent research suggests a more judicious verdict, with achievements as well as failures during this period, not to mention a number of promising innovations. The rise of Napoleon is rendered more problematic – and much more interesting – as a result of these discoveries. Yet there is also a sense in which some of the Directory's successes, most notably in the military sphere, only made the seizure of power by a general more likely, while a series of *coups d'état* left a depoliticized and demoralized citizenry largely indifferent to the overthrow of the liberal Republic.

The Constitution of 1795

The fall of Robespierre on 9 Thermidor of the Year II (27 July 1794) is usually taken as marking the end of the Terror (1793–4). This notorious period of emergency government is chiefly remembered for its repressive machinery which led to some 15,000 executions, countless arrests and hundreds of deaths in custody. Members of parliament like Danton were numbered among the victims, who were drawn from all classes of society. After Thermidor, surviving politicians were confronted with the awesome task of restoring normality, but the foundations of the liberal regime they established have often been condemned as fatally flawed. The deputy Rouault was soon suggesting that the new system contained 'the seeds of its own demise', while several historians have identified congenital weaknesses; according to this interpretation, the downfall of the Directory was the inevitable outcome of the botched Constitution of 1795.

Yet this was the third constitutional document generated during the revolutionary decade and its authors could draw on a great wealth of experience. The National Convention, the parliament originally elected in 1792 to draft a republican constitution after the removal of the king, remained in being for a third year while another new scheme was devised. Those who dominated the assembly after Thermidor, the so-called Thermidorians, comprised repentant terrorists, supporters of the executed Danton, assorted moderates, and deputies who had been forcibly excluded from the Convention in 1793 but were now able to return. They represented a varied but seasoned group of politicians who quite reasonably aimed at devising a liberal constitution within a republican framework, avoiding the pitfalls perceived in both the monarchical Constitution of 1791 and its radical successor, drafted in 1793.

Like its predecessors, the Constitution of 1795 (or the Year III) was prefaced by a fresh edition of the Declaration of the Rights of Man and the Citizen. This famous document had first been drafted as a statement of principle in the summer of 1789 at the outset of the Revolution. To be sure, the rights to education, poor relief and a job, which had appeared in the more radical version of 1793, were removed two years later, together with the 'sacred' rights of insurrection and resistance to oppression. It was explicitly stated in 1795 that 'equality consists solely in the fact that the law is the same for all', an echo of the debate in the Thermidorian Convention where economic equality was denounced as a 'chimera'. More original in 1795 was the addition of a Declaration of Duties, mooted but not drafted in 1789, which stated that 'the obligations of everyone towards society involve defending and serving the *patrie*, submitting to the laws and respecting those who administer them'.

As for the franchise, the infamous distinction between 'active citizens' who could vote and 'passive citizens' who could not, which had caused so much controversy in the early years of the Revolution, was now wisely discarded. The rights of women were not mentioned at all, but all adult male taxpayers were awarded the franchise, some six million Frenchmen in all; only the very poor were excluded. This minimal restriction on voting provoked little adverse comment: the result was a far more generous, basic suffrage than any in Europe. However, a two-stage electoral mechanism was re-established in 1795, instead of the direct parliamentary elections envisaged in 1793, and this erected a very real barrier to democracy.

Voters at the primary level merely chose members of electoral colleges, which met in each of the ninety departments, the basic administrative units of the rapidly expanding Republic (see map of France on p.xii) There were roughly 30,000 second-degree electors in all, a total frequently confused with the far greater number of individuals who were eligible to serve on the departmental assemblies. Second-degree electors were in fact reselected each year from among the million most wealthy males in the population, a substantially larger segment of the wider electorate than is usually acknowledged. Even so, the choice of national deputies was quite deliberately entrusted to the property-owning élite, rather than to the broad, primary electorate. As Boissy d'Anglas, one of the architects of the Constitution, stated in forthright fashion when proposing its adoption in the summer of 1795: 'We must be ruled by the best. The best are the most educated and those most interested in the maintenance of the laws. Now, with very few exceptions, you will find such men only among those possessing property.'

Boissy had been confronted with the severed head of one of his parliamentary colleagues, brandished on a pike and then deposited on the rostrum in front of him, when the Parisian *sans-culottes* had once more invaded the Convention, to press their radical demands, in the spring of 1795. No wonder he also declared: 'A country governed by property-owners is in the social order; one where the propertyless govern is in a state of nature.' For Boissy, as John McManners has commented, the state of nature was no philosophical dream, but the nightmare of anarchy; like most of his Thermidorian colleagues, Boissy was understandably keen to restore stability. The graduated franchise has been condemned as a retreat from democracy, but the two-tier electoral system might be viewed as a realistic device in a society where wealth and education were so unevenly distributed; indirect elections had attracted few objections earlier in the Revolution.

The abandonment of the single-chamber legislature of 1791 and 1793 in favour of two parliamentary chambers was equally the fruit of careful reflection. With the demise of the monarchy, there remained no brake on the actions of a single assembly, and during the Terror the National Convention seemed to have demonstrated just how irresponsible such a body might become. The proposal for two chambers had been made before, but it was now shorn of its aristocratic connotations since both houses were to be elected from among the citizenry as a whole. The Council of Five Hundred formed a lower chamber, which initiated legislation that was submitted for approval (or rejection, but not amendment) to an upper house, the Council of Elders (composed of 250 men aged over forty), before it passed into law. The Legislature was to be renewed by a third each year, in an effort to preserve continuity and avoid any abrupt transformation in the chambers' personnel.

At the helm of the ship of state was a collegial, five-man executive Directory, which gave the regime its name. The Directors themselves were installed in the Luxembourg Palace, a poorly equipped building which was not intended to encourage delusions of grandeur. It was located some distance from the parliamentary assemblies, which were housed in the finer setting of the Tuileries and the Palais Bourbon, on either side of the River Seine (see map of Paris on p.xi). The supremacy of the Legislature was emphasized by the fact that deputies would choose the Directors, who had to be drawn from beyond the ranks of current parliamentarians. In an additional effort to prevent the executive power exceeding its authority, it was stipulated that the Directory would be partially renewed each year and that retiring directors, selected by lot, would not be able to serve in the same capacity again for another five years.

It has often been said that this scheme was too mechanistic for its own good. In the absence of a spirit of co-operation, the separation of powers ordained in 1795 might well induce paralysis, rather than safeguard freedom. The executive Directory was not able to introduce legislation of its own, but merely to make representations to the Council of Five Hundred; nor did the executive have any authority to suspend legislation or dissolve the chambers. The absence of executive agents in the Legislature could easily bring the business of government grinding to a halt, since legislators had no automatic right to dismiss Directors. Deadlock between the two chambers would be difficult to resolve, while cohabitation between opposing majorities on the executive and in parliament would not be easy to achieve; in these circumstances, the Directors might be tempted to resort to illegality to ensure greater compliance from the Councils.

In addition to its control of war and diplomacy, and the right to appoint ministers, the executive Directory was given considerable powers over police and local government. The directorial period is often depicted as a return to decentralization after the attempt to concentrate authority during the Terror. Yet this is a profound misconception, for the balance of power remained tilted firmly towards the centre by the emasculation of rival authority in the localities. The big cities that had proved a law unto themselves – above all Paris – were stripped of their mayors and split into smaller units (in Paris, for example, twelve *arrondissements* were created). At the same time, rural municipalities were amalgamated and the overall number of locally elected posts was substantially reduced.

Moreover, the Directory was given wide powers to dismiss municipal and departmental administrators and override their decisions. It did not hesitate to use this authority, working through executive agents (the *commissaires du pouvoir exécutif*) chosen by the Directory, who were attached to all local bodies. These new officials have, with some exaggeration, been heralded as forerunners of the Napoleonic prefects. The achievements of the Directory in the administrative sphere were certainly substantial, even though they have frequently been overlooked, like other unglamorous but equally important successes with taxation and the monetary system.

Many commentators have bitterly criticized the procedure for constitutional revision that the Thermidorians prescribed. In order to forestall any precipitate change, it was deliberately rendered a long-winded process. Even after three consecutive legislatures had approved revision, it was still necessary to convene a specially elected revisionary chamber and to consult the primary assemblies before reform could be implemented. The objective of permanence in an age of instability was a laudable one, but if a week in politics is a long time, then the nine years demanded for revision was an eternity that few politicians could honestly contemplate. Change came about unconstitutionally after only four years, but hindsight should not be abused: in 1798 the journalist François Poultier published an imaginary report on the Constitution of the Year III celebrating its centenary.

The British have always been inclined to extol the flexibility of an unwritten constitution. Edmund Burke, the eighteenth-century British parliamentarian whose stature had grown with every setback for a Revolution he had denounced from the outset, duly derided this latest attempt at a political settlement in France. It was an extremely lengthy document, comprising 377 articles on justice, the army, finances and education, as well as legislation and administration. Fifteen clauses were devoted to constitutional revision and there was excessive detail on relatively minor points of protocol: for instance, the Directors were obliged to conduct all their official duties dressed in their ceremonial robes designed after the classical fashion by the artist and pageant-master Jacques-Louis David. One appreciates the point that Bonaparte later made when he declared that a constitution should be 'short and obscure'. Yet, given a willingness to make it work, the Constitution of 1795 might have underpinned a viable regime. To be sure, the necessary spirit of political compromise was in desperately short supply after six years of deeply divisive revolutionary upheaval; it remained to be seen if some sort of broad consensus could be created. [**DOCUMENT VI**]

The revolt of the electorate

On paper the 1795 Constitution was not as unreasonable as many historians have suggested. Just because this wordy constitutional document ultimately failed to restore stability, and thus end the Revolution as its authors hoped, does not mean that it was doomed from the outset. Yet the Directory got off to the worst possible start with the inaugural elections of September and October 1795. A storm of protest greeted the decision to restrict the choice of a majority of deputies in the new Legislature to those currently serving in the Convention. Many people wanted the veteran *conventionnels* to retire and take their bad memories of the Terror with them. Instead the will of the people was thwarted, and Albert Goodwin has accordingly suggested that the Directory was born, as well as died, by means of a *coup d'état*.

The Thermidorians were painfully aware of their unpopularity, as 'perpetuals' who had been sitting in the National Convention since 1792. They were rightly fearful that few of them would be returned to the Legislature when the new constitution was put into effect. Hence the infamous device of the law of 'two-thirds', which declared that two-thirds of the new Councils should be selected among existing deputies in the Convention. This decision was justified on the dubious grounds that partial renewal of parliament was prescribed by the Constitution, as well as the more practical argument that to place a new system in the hands of inexperienced deputies was asking for trouble. None the less, the 'two-thirds' was regarded by many voters simply as a ploy for self-perpetuation on the part of politicians unwilling to relinquish power after three years at the helm. Opposition was evident in negative votes cast in the constitutional referendum of September 1795, which overwhelmingly endorsed the Constitution, but revealed widespread hostility to the law of the two-thirds.

Protests culminated in an uprising at Paris on 13 Vendémiaire (5 October 1795), which was led from wealthy western districts in the capital, where all but one electoral district had unanimously rejected the 'unacceptable limitation on the rights of the people' that the law of the two-thirds was deemed to represent. Unlike the earlier insurrections of *sans-culottes*, whose residual power had been removed during the Thermidorian reaction, the Vendémiaire uprising was led by members of the middle classes. Ironically, the rebellious bourgeoisie employed the same rhetoric of direct democracy and local sovereignty to defend their cause as the lower classes had done before them.

The insurgents aimed to exclude long-serving deputies from the Convention and to punish those held responsible for the Terror, rather than to restore the monarchy, at least in the short term. The Thermidorian politicians, however, were in no mood to compromise and they responded sharply. This Parisian uprising, which turned out to be the last of the revolutionary decade, was speedily suppressed by the regular army in an ominous portent of what was to come. Barras, a deputy with military experience, was placed in charge of defending the Convention from attack, and he went to Napoleon for help. Bonaparte, who turned his cannons on the crowd in the famous 'whiff of grapeshot', was able to put an earlier association with Robespierre behind him, and he was rewarded with command of the army in Italy as a result.

After the failure of the insurrection in Paris, the electoral assemblies had no choice but to comply with the law of the two-thirds. The 'new third', freely selected as the voters wished, were mostly of a more right-wing temperament and included some constitutional monarchists who had sat in the two earlier revolutionary parliaments. Even the deputies retained from the Convention were mostly chosen among the more moderate members; there were few regicides among them. Hostility towards former members of the Convention persisted at subsequent elections, so their presence in the directorial Legislature gradually diminished; by 1799 less than a hundred *conventionnels* remained. Still, for the moment, fresh deputies were condemned to minority status in the new legislative councils which, in October 1795, proceeded to elect the first executive Directory.

All but one of the five men chosen as Directors had shown their commitment to the Republic by voting for the execution of the king in 1793 (and the fifth had been absent when the vote was taken). They were all competent administrators, but they were hardly commanding personalities. Sieyès, the great hero of 1789, declined to serve, doubtless deterred by the cold shoulder that his own constitutional proposals had received. The most popular candidate was La Revellière-Lépeaux, a dour anticlerical who hailed from the west of France. He was accompanied by Reubell, who came from Alsace and was a determined anti-Jacobin; Carnot, the army officer dubbed 'the organizer of victory' in 1793 and a former member of the Committee of Public Safety which had led France to military success during the Terror; Letourneur, an engineer with naval expertise but few ideological convictions; and, finally, Barras, an opportunistic former nobleman from Provence. Barras was a capable if cynical politician, who gave the regime a somewhat undeserved reputation for corruption. He was still in post when the Directory was overthrown in 1799, by the same General Bonaparte who had helped to establish it in Vendémiaire 1795.

The royalist challenge

It was a sign of the times that Paris, once a hotbed of left-wing agitation, should produce a right-wing uprising at the inception of the Directory. Alfred Cobban suggested that a royalist restoration appeared the most likely outcome after Thermidor, so the success of the Directory in containing royalism might be seen as one of its major achievements. Of course, the terminology employed by the regime itself to describe conservative opponents should not be taken at face value. Not all so-called 'royalists', who continued to represent the major threat to the regime during the first two years of the Directory, were necessarily in favour of an immediate monarchical restoration. Indeed, disagreement among those who favoured the return of a king explains their lack of success as much as republican resolve. Above all, they lacked the crucial ingredient for a palatable royalist recipe, namely, a serious pretender who was prepared to compromise with the Revolution.

When the infant son of Louis XVI (the so-called Louis XVII) died in captivity in Paris in 1795, the comte de Provence, Louis XVI's younger brother, claimed the throne as Louis XVIII. His subsequent Declaration from Verona, where he was currently residing in exile, was a great disappointment to the majority of his potential subjects, for it offered few concessions to revolutionary principles: 'It is essential to restore the form of government which has ensured the greatness of France for more than fourteen centuries', it stated. [**DOCUMENT VII**] It promised to investigate 'abuses' in the old order, but the threat to restore 'stolen properties' was sufficient to alienate not just purchasers of *biens nationaux*, but also all those who had benefited from the abolition of tithes and seigneurial dues. Louis XVIII may have felt that compromise was irrelevant because the Republic was on the verge of collapse, but the document reveals just how out of touch he had become.

Should he return, there would obviously be reprisals against republicans in general and regicides in particular, but constitutional monarchists also despaired; the future Louis XVIII had so far failed to forget or learn very much at all. Some conservatives accordingly placed their hopes in the Orleanist branch of the French royal family. This option was attractive to former Jacobins as well as to constitutional monarchists, because the duke of Orleans had participated in the Revolution until he came to grief in 1793. His son, Louis-Philippe, had fought in the revolutionary army before he too fell under suspicion and emigrated in 1793. He was presumably prepared to compromise with 'the principles of 1789', but resolutely refused any political role and departed for America in 1796 (though he would later return and eventually lead the July Monarchy after 1830).

Many sympathizers with the monarchical ideal were reluctant to seek a violent overthrow of the Republic. They dissociated themselves from hardened counter-revolutionaries, like the ill-fated band who landed at Quiberon Bay in the west of France in July 1795, only to be met by republican forces who massacred them on the spot. Royalist extremists of this sort, including the sizeable contingent of noble *émigrés*, pinned their hopes on assistance from abroad. English agents were prepared to lavish considerable amounts of money on attempts to co-ordinate enemy invasion with internal uprisings, but the various conspiracies they hatched, though real and alarming, rarely came to fruition. Indeed, the association of royalism with foreign powers jarred with the patriotism of many directorial opponents.

Links with endemic peasant insurrection were equally difficult for royalist agents to forge. Rebellious country-folk or *chouans* in western France, in the former provinces of Brittany and Normandy, were far from being devoted subjects of the king. Like the peasants who had fought in the great uprising in the Vendée in 1793, they pursued their own agenda of hostility to larger landowners and townspeople, besides revealing a staunch allegiance to the old-regime Church. Their revolt really aimed at combating those forces – governmental, religious and economic – that threatened their traditional way of life. Theirs was essentially a local revolt, a form of 'resistance' to the Revolution, rather than outright counter-revolution aimed at a return to the old order. It rendered them unreliable and also unwelcome allies for most constitutional monarchists.

Rural unrest like *chouannerie* easily degenerated into banditry, and the same could be said of the brutal White Terror, or Counter-Terror, that raged in the south of France and was chiefly directed against former Jacobin militants. As soon as prisoners were released after Thermidor, revenge killings began, though it is often difficult to see a clear political motive behind some of these murders. The number of victims under the Directory certainly numbered thousands, though precise figures are impossible to obtain since this was unofficial, unlicensed violence, unlike the Terror of 1793. Former members of republican watch committees and revolutionary tribunals were not even safe in gaol, for there were some appalling prison massacres at Lyons and Marseilles in 1795. Evidently the deep wounds opened earlier in the Revolution would be hard to heal, but anarchical expressions of popular royalism did not commend themselves to the élites and were impossible to incorporate into any coherent campaign for a restoration of the monarchy.

Moderate 'royalists' instead sought to take power legally by grasping the electoral opportunities and press freedoms that the

Constitution now offered. They had the backing of businessmen, especially in the great ports where commerce had been ruined by the war against the maritime powers. Middle-class property-owners in general were deeply suspicious of the Republic. They had supported the Revolution of 1789 and profited from the sale of *biens nationaux*, but they had since been physically threatened by the Terror and remained deeply suspicious of the Directory's claim to restore political and social order. Individuals like these, the so-called *honnêtes gens* or well-to-do folk, required reassurance that the Republic would indeed be a conservative one and they wanted guarantees against any resurgence of Jacobin radicalism.

In order to contest parliamentary elections in the spring of 1797, conservative deputies and journalists gathered at the Club de Clichy in Paris and set up institutes in some of the major provincial cities. Their electoral strategy briefly won over the more intransigent elements and even Louis XVIII was persuaded to give his blessing to the campaign. When their success at the polls was met by expulsion from the Legislature, some were forced to revert to clandestine or subversive activities, yet others continued to exploit the opportunities for legal opposition that remained open to them. They were still a force to be reckoned with in 1799. So were the *émigrés*, who would not renounce their counter-revolutionary endeavours as long as they remained in exile. *Chouannerie* too persisted, a running sore exacerbated by the insatiable demands of the Republic for men and money, and by the continuing persecution of priests.

Religion and the Republic

Much of the residual strength of 'royalism', or more properly political conservatism, lay among those who remained loyal to Catholicism. Yet article 354 of the Constitution of 1795 stated, 'No one can be prevented from exercising, within the laws, the religion of their choice', and added, 'no one can be forced to contribute to the upkeep of any church. The Republic does not recognize or pay for any religion.' Such a separation of Church and state had been unthinkable a few years earlier, and it held out the prospect of religious pluralism and freedom for the individual worshipper, in place of the persecution that had prevailed during the Terror.

The attempt to reform the Church in the early years of the Revolution, in order to align it with the new regime, had been a major cause of divided loyalties since 1791. Those who refused to accept the Civil Constitution of the Clergy, passed by the National Assembly in 1790, became known as 'refractories' or 'non-jurors', since they had refused to swear an oath of allegiance to the new system. Most of the old-regime bishops went into exile, but dissident lower clergy, who comprised roughly half the parish priests, stayed on. They were strongly entrenched in the west, the Massif Central and the north-east, where they took their parishioners with them into opposition to the Revolution as a whole. From 1792 onwards, refractory priests were liable to imprisonment and deportation, but the juring or constitutional clergy, who continued to work as salaried (though in practice unpaid) servants of the state, were soon abandoned by the revolutionaries.

All religious affiliations came to be regarded as a potential threat to the Republic. Indeed, the Revolution took on an increasingly anti-Christian aura, symbolized by the new calendar adopted in 1793 which abolished Sundays and religious festivals and encouraged the worship of reason instead. A wave of 'dechristianization' swept through certain parts of France, leaving churches closed and congregations lacking priests, many of whom had been forced into hiding or had been encouraged to marry and renounce their clerical vows. The origins of this phenomenon are extremely complex, with deep roots in popular anticlericalism. Yet the prevailing climate of war and civil war was evidently instrumental in unleashing hostility towards priests in general, who were widely regarded as counter-revolutionaries in religious garb.

As the Terror drew to a close, the Thermidorians abandoned persecution, and Christians began to worship openly again. Inevitably there was a rush in 1795 to seize the renewed opportunity to take the sacraments at services offered by both constitutional and refractory clergy, who emerged from hiding or returned from exile. It has been estimated that churches were soon reopened in over two-thirds of French towns and villages. It was often women who led the way to reclaim churches to be reconsecrated for religious use, pestering officials to hand over keys and then restoring the premises from their frequently dilapidated condition. The directorial authorities were deeply worried about this new-found enthusiasm for worship, and many priests discovered that their most assiduous communicants were actually police spies. Republican fears were compounded by the re-emergence of religious schools, which offered a Christian dimension conspicuously lacking in state institutions and threatened to 'pervert' the minds of the rising generation.

The constitutional Church sought to rebuild its shattered framework, engaging in some innovations in the process: part of the Mass was conducted in French and bishops were elected by the faithful. In the absence of enough ordained priests, there was a good deal of lay involvement in conducting services, not to mention public worship for the Protestant and Jewish minorities. One historian has recently hailed the diversity of practice permitted in 1795 and 1796 as a great experiment far in advance of its time. Yet religious 'pluralism' had little appeal for most contemporaries. More to the point, it failed to impress the Directory, which was unable to abandon republican animosity towards any sort of religious revival.

Few politicians could accept the idea of state neutrality in Church affairs, or consider religious practice a purely personal matter. Severe limitations continued to be imposed upon the clergy, who were not allowed to wear distinctive clothing, while religious ceremonies were confined to church buildings. Processions, pilgrimages and the ringing of bells were strictly forbidden. Grégoire, a courageous bishop who was attempting to reorganize the remaining constitutional clergy, was moved to comment that 'the liberty of religious practice exists in Turkey, but it does not exist in France'. Additional oaths of allegiance were soon imposed upon the priesthood. Many clergymen, even refractories, were prepared to swear them, on the grounds that the Christian religion could coexist with any form of government. Yet those who refused were clearly courting disaster, putting themselves outside the law and paving the way for further persecution, which was not slow to materialize.

Grudging, official toleration did not last long before the 'royalist' upsurge in the elections of the Year V (spring 1797) reinforced the religious revival, which now had plenty of support within the legislative body. There were, for example, proposals to repeal the divorce laws and relax measures against refractory priests. When measures were taken to curb 'royalism' in September 1797, it was no surprise to find religious repression returning as well. A new oath of 'hatred of royalty' was imposed, which made even those with tough consciences pause before they took it, while the Directory was empowered to punish refractories by administrative fiat. Literally thousands of priests were rounded up and, though few were executed, some 200 were sent to the penal colony of Guiana in South America where most died of fever. Hundreds more were imprisoned in dreadful conditions on the prison hulks at Rochefort, or on the nearby islands of Ré and Oléron off the west coast of France.

Nor was there much enthusiasm for revolutionary cults, such as Theophilanthropy, which were based on an intellectual celebration of nature and the supreme being, but had little popular appeal. After 1798, the Republic instituted official celebrations as a kind of civic religion and made a determined effort to enforce the revolutionary calendar. Not surprisingly, there was little welcome for a ten-day week that offered fewer days of repose than the traditional Christian dispensation. Saints' days disappeared along with Christmas and Easter, and the attempt to replace them with republican festivals, evoking not just the great days of the Revolution but also youth, marriage and old age, cut little ice with the general public. As John McManners puts it, 'In the battered churches, only unwilling officials, recalcitrant children, impatient marriage parties and stray dogs turned up to hear the reading of the *Bulletin* [the latest laws] and perfunctory martial music.'

In practice, then, the Directory was unable to replace Christianity or transcend the intolerant approach of its predecessors. Despite the efforts of a committed republican clergyman like the abbé Grégoire, Catholics were inevitably alienated from the regime. In the process, the Directory was offering hostages to 'royalism', which alone seemed to hold out the possibility of a return to religious order. The failure of the revolutionary cults only served to point up the usefulness of an established Church to both state and society. Some republicans, such as those who had pacified the west with promises of freedom of worship, were aware of the need for a settlement, but they were unable to persuade enough of their colleagues, who were proving as fanatical as the Christians they so fervently denounced. Nor did they heed the warning uttered by the deputy Boulay de la Meurthe, just a few months before Brumaire, that anyone prepared to establish religious freedom would prove extremely popular.

The Jacobin revival

Royalism is not easy to pin down during the Directory, and 'Jacobins', or 'anarchists' as they were usually styled in government propaganda, present similar problems of definition. Of course, these were loaded terms deliberately employed by the authorities to conjure up visions of the Terror and to frighten people. What is more, the Babeuf plot of 1796, which was inspired by a primitive version of socialism, made it possible for the Directory to tar left-wing opponents with the brush of communism. **[DOCUMENT VIII]** In fact, most Jacobins during the directorial period were proponents of a property-owning democracy. They appealed to the lower classes, especially in the towns and, above all, in Paris, by seeking to expand the franchise and extend the opportunities for education and employment. Their leaders were mostly middle-class professional men, who sought power in order to combat refractory priests and returning *émigrés* as much as to threaten the established social order.

Historians like Isser Woloch, who has demonstrated the importance of the Jacobin revival under the Directory, accordingly prefer the label 'neo-Jacobin' (though this was not used at the time) in order to distinguish these radicals from their allegedly more doctrinaire predecessors in 1793. Jacobinism was never a coherent ideology, and the network of clubs on which the movement had been based was destroyed in the wake of Robespierre's downfall in 1794. There were sporadic attempts to revive societies of a similar type in 1795, but the executive Directory moved swiftly to suppress the slightest hint of any political association. The Babeuf plot of 1796, which pursued a conspiratorial approach in order to avoid discovery, was a reflection of the scant popular support that former Jacobins were now able to muster. The imposition of a new order from above seemed to have replaced the vision of a people seizing power for themselves from below. Yet the conspiracy proved an abject failure. Its historical reputation was salvaged by the stout defence of his actions that Babeuf offered at his trial, before he was executed and turned into a martyr.

There has been much discussion of the ideas involved in the planned insurrection and of the extent to which fellow conspirators were aiming at some kind of communism rather than an application of the democratic Constitution of 1793. Whatever the truth, the practical effect of the failure of the Babeuf plot was to encourage radicals to seek alternative strategies. Left-wingers, like their counterparts on the right, now rejected violence and sought to work through the existing political system. They were given greater latitude to do so after the Directory was thrown into panic by 'royalist' successes at the polls in 1797. In the wake of the crack-down on the right that followed, political clubs began to reappear as 'constitutional circles', a label specifically designed to indicate a commitment to upholding the Constitution of 1795.

The major objective of these latter-day Jacobin clubs was victory at the polls in the elections of the Year VI, to be held in the spring of

1798. To this end, aided and abetted by sympathetic local authorities and assisted by newspapers like the *Journal des hommes libres de tous les pays*, they began a campaign of propaganda and organization that was especially successful in departments of the west, centre and south-west, where the threat from 'royalism' was most evident and where republican resistance appeared to need stiffening. The Directory, which had initially welcomed this Jacobin revival as a counterweight to the royalist thrust of 1797, now found that it was facing defeat from the opposite quarter. Its response was to issue warrants for the closure of constitutional circles and their associated newspapers in many areas.

By then it was too late, so electoral results favourable to the Jacobins were subsequently annulled, usually on the pretext that regulations had been flouted at the assemblies. Yet the wider movement of circles and newspapers survived here and there, in different shapes and forms, and preparations were put in hand for the elections of the following year. Indeed, in the early summer of 1799 the Jacobin revival was given fresh impetus by the relaxation of repressive legislation. Numerous clubs re-emerged, including one in Paris. The Jacobins, who were historically associated with emergency government and Terror, had now become ardent defenders of the Constitution of 1795. To be sure, the Constitution left a good deal to be desired from a democratic point of view, but it offered the best available means of opposing both royalism and the corrupt rule of a self-perpetuating, middle-class oligarchy. [**DOCUMENT IX**]

Economic and social difficulties

It would be wrong to suggest that Jacobins were the only beneficiaries of the popular discontent that plagued the Directory. The difficult conditions that marked, or rather marred, the early years of the regime could be exploited by the right as easily as by the left. Whatever the political consequences, the Directory has always been depicted as a time of economic and social breakdown. According to Frédéric Masson, for example:

> What flourished in France when Bonaparte took control in the *coup* of Brumaire? Almost nothing. For ten years, factional strife and foreign and civil war had forced the succession of governments that came and went to live hand to mouth . . . the country was completely devastated and only a strong man could put France back on its feet.

The situation was rather more nuanced than the 'black legend' of Bonapartist propaganda would suggest. The beginning of the Directory unfortunately coincided with some appalling weather during the terrible winter of the Year III (1794–5), which was among the most severe of the eighteenth century. The harvest of 1794 had been a poor one, so peasants were reluctant to part with their meagre crops. By December, on account of the intense cold, transport had completely ground to a halt; the River Seine, for example, froze all the way from Rouen to Paris. The resulting combination of food shortage and low temperatures was a lethal one. Deaths, chiefly among the very young and the elderly, rose to twice their normal levels, and in 1796 mortality remained abnormally high in many parts of France as a weakened population succumbed to a series of epidemics.

The regime could scarcely be blamed for poor climatic conditions, but the situation was certainly made much worse by the return to the free market. Liberated from the constraints of the Terror which had temporarily stopped the rot, paper money (the infamous *assignats*) resumed their alarming depreciation and prices rocketed, putting them way beyond the means of ordinary wage-earners in the cities. Since their introduction in 1791, the *assignats* had failed to inspire confidence, but by the end of 1795 they had become practically worthless. Hyper-inflation set in: bread, which normally sold at roughly two or three *sols* a pound, rose towards 100 *sols*. The Directory conducted an ill-fated experiment with another type of paper money, the *mandats territoriaux*, introduced in 1796, but these bills ran the same course as the *assignats* within a few months. There was no alternative but to return to hard cash, though the restoration of monetary confidence would prove a protracted process.

In 1793 the Jacobins had attempted, albeit without much success, to curb inflation by means of the celebrated 'Maximum', a series of controls on prices and wages. In an effort to entice goods on to the open market, the Thermidorians abolished the Maximum at the end of 1794. Pressure from local authorities and the threat of rioting ensured that controls remained on bread prices, though in many cities the bread ration was reduced to less than a pound per person per day, and it was also increasingly expensive. Other foodstuffs reappeared, but at prices beyond the pockets of the ordinary buyer. In Paris, for example, pâté, ham and cherries were available for purchase in the early spring of 1795, while the poor were quite literally starving. The wealthy returning home from banquets and balls in the early hours of the morning could see the bread queues beginning to form, despite the sub-zero temperatures.

The widening gap between rich and poor has undoubtedly coloured images of the Directory. Yet it should be remembered that, apart from the brief Jacobin ascendancy of the Year II, the Revolution had only aimed to strip away privileges of birth, not inequalities of fortune. Careers open to talents were intended to facilitate the rise of able individuals, while the sale of *biens nationaux*, and later tenders for war contracts, created opportunities for spectacular enrichment. Under the Directory, puritanical attitudes towards wealth and display were abandoned along with Robespierre's Republic of Virtue. During the Terror it was decidedly unwise to flaunt one's riches, but now there was no longer any reason to be ashamed of luxury or personal indulgence. The period was equally notorious for the antics of society hostesses, such as Madame Tallien or Joséphine de Beauharnais, the future wife of Napoleon. As Martyn Lyons has put it,

> Thus, the traditional French bourgeois was joined, and in the capital thrown into the shadows, by parvenu elements who found a faster way to wealth and success and were not afraid to show it. Their wealth was paraded ostentatiously, and the mores of high society were liberal to the point of licence . . .

At the other end of the scale, the poor found themselves deprived of the facilities for survival that had existed under the old regime. It was one thing to promise the right to work and public assistance, as the 1793 version of the Rights of Man had done, but in practice the Revolution had dislocated the existing 'welfare' infrastructure without creating any viable alternative. The Church was no longer in a position to play its traditional charitable role, while inflation had ravaged the bequests on which many philanthropic institutions depended, and the government was unable to fill the gap. Conditions for those obliged to rely on foundling homes, hospitals or almshouses were truly dreadful, though there are some indications that, with the return of some financial stability and administrative order towards the end of the decade, the poor were being treated a little less badly.

It should be stressed that economic conditions began to improve soon after the Directory was established. A bumper harvest in 1796, followed by two more good years in 1797 and 1798, removed the threat of famine. Despite the deflationary effects of the return to metallic currency which hit rural producers especially hard, by the end of the 1790s economic activity was beginning to recover. Surveys ordered by Napoleon in 1800 paint a rather blacker picture of the directorial years than is warranted, for circumstances took a turn for the worse again in 1799, with the renewed impact of war and another adverse bout of weather: the Consulate came to power in the midst of a fresh economic crisis. To be sure, the internal network of roads and canals was in poor shape, while the once thriving ports were crippled by the British naval blockade, and industrial production remained well below the level of 1789. The revolutionary decade of upheaval and war had inevitably taken a heavy toll. On the other hand, manufacturing was coming out of recession, assisted by a government which organized the first national exhibition for industry in 1798. The leading specialist on the directorial economy concludes that a good basis was being laid for the future development; once again Bonaparte would reap where the Directory had sown.

Poverty and distress do not in themselves bring down regimes. Despite, or perhaps because of, the difficult circumstances experienced in the late 1790s, the era of urban insurrection was over. Unrest was still endemic in the countryside, and widespread misery did induce a climate of insecurity reflected in high levels of crime and other types of antisocial behaviour. Yet at worst popular suffering resulted in apathy and indifference towards the regime, which was not immediately threatening to its existence. In the longer run, however, it left the Directory dangerously exposed and, in the absence of popular support or sufficient commitment from the middle classes, reliant on illegal measures for its survival.

The regime of the coup d'état

One novel feature of the new regime, as advocated in the 1793 Constitution and actually introduced in 1795, was the practice of regular, annual elections. The objective was a laudable one. It was widely believed that periodic, complete renewal of the legislature and the local administration would produce abrupt change and need-lessly forfeit the accumulated wisdom of experienced deputies. Instead, the annual elections employed to tackle this difficulty, and conduct a steady apprenticeship in electoral politics, created perennial instability. In the words of one journalist, opening the polls was tantamount to taking the lid off Pandora's Box and unleashing all kinds of anarchy. As soon as the consequences of one partial renewal had been dealt with, it was necessary to begin thinking about the next round scheduled for the following spring.

Napoleon's solution was to emasculate the electoral process, though not to abolish it. Many of the addresses sent to his provisional government in the wake of the *coup* of Brumaire criticized this particular aspect of the Constitution of 1795. 'Frequent electoral assemblies' were invoked as a recipe for disaster: 'they brought trouble for two months beforehand and two months afterwards', asserted one correspondent, while another suggested that 'the country is in a state of agitation for at least half the year'. The stipulation that members of the departmental electoral colleges were not eligible the following year only increased the element of instability that was repeated at all levels of the electoral process. For all elected bodies, departmental and municipal, as well as the executive Directory itself, were subject to the same system of annual partial renewal and restricted re-eligibility.

The frequency of elections and the rapid turnover of personnel might not have caused such havoc had there been more unity among the voters, especially those eligible to serve as second-degree electors. In fact, even among the wealthy élite which controlled the electoral colleges that met annually in each of the ninety-odd departments, there was such hostility to the regime that the Constitution itself seemed perpetually threatened. The centre would not hold and either 'royalists' or 'Jacobins', each of whom posed a fundamental challenge to the regime, were elected in significant numbers, rather than 'directorialists' wholly committed to upholding the system.

The problem was that electoral contests reopened political wounds which the Directory was unable to heal. The stakes of the political game were extremely high. Six years of Revolution, especially the last two or three, had inevitably left a residue of hatred that made it difficult for former opponents to accept the electoral triumph of those responsible for seizing their property and killing their relatives. There were too many pasts to be lived down, and the Directory's search for dispassionate administrators who would secure general acceptance, especially at the local level, was doomed to disappointment in many parts of the country.

As the directorial commissioner at Marseilles, a commercial port especially prone to division and disorder throughout the decade, put it:

> When the life-blood of all the parties has been frequently spilled and remains fresh, in the midst of assassins and their victims, how can one

> find disinterested candidates for office . . . everyone puts forward and wishes to see elected the accomplices of his furious deeds, or at least weak citizens who can be easily influenced. Are there any families who do not have some political skeletons in the cupboard?

The Directory frequently struggled to find 'committed, decent, firm republicans, who would be enemies of all types of faction'. Aulard once suggested that 'the nation handed in its resignation' when many of the elected personnel simply refused to serve. Given the perils of holding office, this reluctance to take up posts as municipal councillors or justices of the peace is hardly surprising. Yet the Directory contributed to the problem by overturning election results and inserting its own nominees. At Aix-en-Provence, an administrative centre not very far from Marseilles, the executive purged the town council twice in 1798 before reinstating the original office-holders.

Historians have repeatedly cited low turn-out in elections under the Directory as an indication of the regime's failure to attract popular support. As a recent history of Normandy during the French Revolution puts it:

> An analysis of electoral returns from 1795 to 1798, reveals a process of disaffection. The mass of the people shunned political activities . . . In these circumstances the revision of the Constitution was as much the secret wish of the nation as the intention of a small number of conspirators preparing a *coup d'état* in Paris.

In fact, in the context of an infant democracy, electoral turn-out under the Directory remained relatively high.

In the Years V and VI (1797 and 1798), over one-quarter of the huge primary electorate was involved, and some towns recorded figures well in excess of that. Apart from 1790, when revolutionary enthusiasm was running high and the country was reasonably peaceful, electoral participation rarely exceeded an average level of 20 per cent. In 1799, in the wake of two successive years when the Directory had flagrantly interfered with the results, attendance at the polls was understandably rather lower, frequently falling towards 10 per cent. Yet it was by no means inevitable that this slump would not be reversed the following year, especially after laws passed in the early summer of 1799 seemed to promise freer elections in the future.

The executive Directory was criticized for the campaigns it mounted to secure satisfactory election results, though it made sense for the government to encourage the return of its own supporters to the legislative Councils. When such efforts proved unsuccessful, however, the Directory and its parliamentary allies simply resorted to illegality, or at best dubious expedients. Such were the repeated violations of its own rules that the Directory has been dubbed the regime of the *coup d'état*. The tradition of insurrection overthrowing the existing order from below, as in 1789 or 1792, was thus supplanted by interference from above to uphold the incumbent regime. Bonaparte could claim that the Constitution was already dead and that he was simply providing a suitable burial, though he would continue to violate the system in a similar fashion himself. Many would argue that the purge of parliament undertaken on 18 Fructidor V (4 September 1797) effectively ended the constitutional experiment of 1795 after only two years. It is often said that the distance separating 18 Fructidor from 18 Brumaire was but a short, inevitable step.

Since the initial legislative elections of Vendémiaire IV (October 1795) were deemed to have 'anticipated' those of 1796, the Directory enjoyed a breathing-space of eighteen months before it was obliged to face the electorate again in Germinal V (March 1797). Yet this delay only earned a stay of execution. As many politicians feared, the elections of spring 1797 witnessed the triumph of right-wing opponents of the regime in a majority of departments. Only eleven retiring legislators who had sat in the National Convention were re-elected and they were now compelled to confront incoming 'royalists' like Imbert-Colomès, a counter-revolutionary agent from Lyons, or the comte de Fleurieu, who had served as a minister under Louis XVI in 1790. More moderate conservatives were frightened by the success of the hard-liners, yet they combined to elect Barthélemy, a former nobleman and old-regime diplomat, to the executive Directory. With sympathizers such as General Pichegru becoming president of the Council of Five Hundred and Barbé-Marbois chairing the Elders, they began to press for a relaxation of laws against *émigrés* and priests and to call for international peace.

This was intolerable to three members of the executive Directory, the 'triumvirate' of Reubell, La Revellière-Lépeaux and Barras, who had no legitimate means of curbing the conservative upsurge and therefore resorted to a *coup*. Hoche, who was made minister of war, sent troops marching towards Paris, in contravention of the 'constitutional radius' intended to keep them out. They infiltrated the capital on the evening of 17 Fructidor V (3 September 1797). General Augereau, who was acting with the permission of Bonaparte, then in Italy, took command of the Paris division, occupied the Councils (in a foretaste of Brumaire) and arrested leading 'royalists'. Fifty-three deputies were deported, together with the Director Barthélemy (Carnot, the fifth Director, managed to escape) and election results were annulled in no fewer than forty-nine departments. A series of repressive laws was unleashed against right-wing sympathizers, *émigrés* and priests in what has become known as the Fructidorian Terror.

The Directory had lived to fight another day, though at the cost of undermining the constitutional legitimacy on which it rested. It might be argued that the royalist threat would have brought down the entire regime. The staunch republican scientist Cabanis wrote: 'The government has saved the Republic . . . The Constitution has not been violated an instant, except in order to save it.' Yet it was only possible to defeat the right by encouraging the left, and a year later the government found that it was once again facing defeat at the polls. As a result of the vacancies left unfilled after the *coup* of Fructidor there were over 400 seats in contention, over half the places in the legislature. Only belatedly did the government realize the extent of the defeat it was facing, but this time it decided to act before too many Jacobin deputies took their seats in Paris. [**DOCUMENT X**]

The so-called *coup d'état* of 22 Floréal VI (11 May 1798) was a means of repeating by legislation what had been achieved by military force the previous year. The existing Councils used the pretext of divisions within the departmental electoral assemblies (where hostile minorities had seceded from the proceedings and then conducted their own separate elections) as a means of annulling unwelcome results in almost half the country. The blatantly partisan approach of the executive is shown by the fact that in several cases the work of small minorities was endorsed. Once again, local elections were treated in a similar fashion: along with 106 deputies, some 200 departmental administrators were removed. Jourdan commented: 'From now on deputies are to be appointed by the executive. The Republic is finished. It is obvious that a regime that systematically nullifies elections in order to create an assembly that pleases the government is no longer a republic, it is a dictatorship.'

The historian Isser Woloch agrees. In his opinion, since they were committed republicans, the Jacobins represented a legitimate opposition, who did not pose a direct threat to the regime in the way that 'royalists' did in 1797. The parliamentary purge of Floréal VI

(May 1798) was thus the critical moment in the history of the Directory, for it showed that the government would tolerate no alternatives to its own interpretation of who should govern France. This time the army was not involved, but the Directory had resorted to legal chicanery even though the regime itself was not at risk, merely its leadership. The possibility of pluralism was denied and the Directory was doomed to some sort of authoritarian outcome because it was not willing to end the Revolution on a more liberal basis.

The extent to which the *coup* of Floréal cut short the development of party politics is currently a matter of debate. A pluralism of sorts had come into being with the Directory, and it was reflected in the robust development of political journalism, as well as in the emergence of competing political associations. The *politique de bascule*, or see-saw politics, that the government had adopted to combat first one and then another set of opponents to its right and left, has often been condemned as feebleness. It might instead be interpreted as an acknowledgement that a 'public space' existed in which rival policies could be legitimately pursued. Press freedom was, however, severely restricted in the wake of the Fructidor *coup* in September 1797 and there was a deep reluctance to recognize the existence of 'factions', as political parties were pejoratively called.

When Bonaparte came to power, he claimed to stand above the party arena and vowed to crush the factions. Any lingering hope of continuing the experiment with pluralistic politics thus ended. The Directory itself had been unwilling to compromise with constitutional opponents on both left and right, a refusal which left only a narrow basis for the construction of a viable, consensual system. The myth of the single, united will, dissent from which represented betrayal, proved too potent for the emergent, liberal alternative. The 'agreement to disagree' is part of a political culture which requires plenty of time to grow and in the brief period that had elapsed since 1795 it enjoyed no more than a charmed existence. Needless to say, the cultivation of democracy was not assisted by the continuing international struggle with the major powers of Europe; the directorial regime was increasingly reliant upon the army, both at home and abroad.

The Republic of bayonets

It has been said that the Directory was a regime attempting to operate normally under abnormal circumstances. It is difficult enough to govern without consensus, but it is wellnigh impossible to sustain a liberal regime while pursuing extensive warfare. The Directory inherited a conflict with a coalition comprising most of the European powers, and commentators such as Aulard have seen this as a key to its collapse. The opportunity to achieve peace with honour in 1797, when only Britain remained belligerent, was missed. The regime proved incapable of living without the war on which it had come to rely for both income and prestige. Yet the continuation of the war carried a permanent risk of defeat, and the victories of the renewed anti-French alliance in 1799 threw the Directory's ability to defend the Republic into serious doubt. Above all, reliance upon the generals for salvation brought the threat of militarization: the army that assisted the foundation and preservation of the Republic might become its grave-digger.

Little by little the Republic's 'citizen' army had become professionalized. Until 1798, when a new law introduced conscription to France (as opposed to the 'one-off' *levée en masse*, or wholesale mobilization, of 1793), the army contained veterans of several years' standing who spent most of their time campaigning outside France. When they did return to the country, their impression of life under the Directory was of a corrupt society, dominated by the pursuit of profit and by hard-faced men who had done well out of the war. They felt alienated from civilians incapable of comprehending the sacrifices they had endured in the course of the lengthy campaigns. For them the Republic was more effectively incarnated in their own ranks and in the person of their generals.

As each army became detached from the *patrie*, so it tended to become a praetorian guard, devoted to its general; it was not only Bonaparte who developed a particular *esprit de corps* through his control of patronage, promotion and pillage. The cult of various military personalities brought the formation of states within states. In Italy, commented one officer, we have 'neither law nor government: the generals are our sovereigns'. These generals became used to operating independently as diplomats and administrators in the occupied territories, like Bonaparte in northern Italy. The efforts of the Directors to keep the military in check, chiefly by means of civilian *commissaires* who were attached to each army, were unsuccessful. There was little that the politicians could do when the regime was so dependent upon the material and monetary assistance that the generals provided.

The Directory had come to rely upon the army, not only to prosecute a war without end, but also to provide internal security.

This was most evident in the role which the army played in the *coup d'état* of 1797, but regular troops were increasingly employed as a peace-keeping force to suppress disorder within France. The civilian police were reorganized under a separate ministry in 1796, but they proved incapable of coping with the breakdown of law and order under the Directory. Brigandage, a fearful brew of mugging, burglary and highway robbery that mixed political opposition with antisocial behaviour, produced a major crime wave. The problem was that measures adopted to promote liberty seemed to work against security. The alternative was to promote security and jeopardize liberty by utilizing troops as a heavily armed police force.

The Fructidor *coup* provided the spur to action since, having violated the Constitution to expel putative royalists, there was less compunction about adopting authoritarian methods for restoring order. Instead of the ineffective *gendarmerie*, army units reinforced by civilian militia (the national guards) were formed into flying columns to comb the countryside and round up bandits. In the towns, military commanders took charge of police matters by declaring a state of siege. The provision was widely used, not to say abused: in the south of France most of the major cities were controlled in this manner after Fructidor. One general replied to criticisms of the device by stating:

> The ill-intentioned keep saying that a town under a state of siege is, so to speak, outside the Constitution; but the Constitution would be meaningless if . . . police powers were in the hands of men who have successively taken turns being the oppressors and the oppressed. The commander of a town under a state of siege will uphold the government's views and preserve peace.

Yet it was not simply a question of deterring offences or apprehending criminals; it was also a matter of trying and punishing them. The system of elected judges and juries, which the Constitution of 1795 had maintained, was unworkable in many parts of directorial France. Convictions for 'political' offences were difficult to obtain in the courts as a result of intimidation and partisan affiliations. Recourse was thus made to the military commissions previously employed under the Terror. At least 700 returned *émigrés* and refractory priests were tried in this manner after the *coup* of Fructidor (September 1797), and many of them were summarily executed. So successful was this form of 'justice' that it was extended to

encompass ordinary criminals. With the passage of further legislation in January 1798, soldiers serving as magistrates in military
courts began dealing with all kinds of serious offences.

The army on which the Republic relied had also become
intimately involved in the parliamentary system, aided and abetted
by many civilian politicians. When public candidatures for office were
briefly permitted in 1797, the names of generals were frequently
submitted, including that of Napoleon Bonaparte. A number of
military leaders were actually elected to the Legislature, a change of
vocation from soldier to parliamentarian that was warmly welcomed
in the cases of Jourdan and Augereau. Several generals, such as
Brune and Masséna, were unsuccessfully nominated to the executive,
and in 1799 General Moulin actually succeeded in becoming a
Director. Perhaps Bonaparte would have been satisfied with promotion of this sort, but unfortunately for him he fell well below the
qualifying age of forty.

Could the Republic survive in these circumstances? John
McManners has suggested that an alternative future for the First
Republic, apart from the Brumaire *coup*, is impossible to envisage.
On the contrary, besides pointing to the successes and vitality of the
Republic, recent research has highlighted a revival of liberal as well as
Jacobin republicanism in the spring of 1799. The elections of the Year
VII, which took place as usual in March and April, were poorly
attended on the whole, and there were numerous schisms at the
departmental assemblies. Yet on this occasion, although the outcome
was unwelcome to the executive Directory, there were no annul-
ments or expulsions. On the contrary, the work of the majority in the
electoral assemblies was systematically endorsed by the validating
committees of the Legislature. More importantly, measures were
being taken to ensure that such manipulation of the electoral
assemblies would not be tolerated in future, while there was renewed
press freedom, and additional liberty was granted to political
associations.

It is possible to read this as a new departure for the Directory,
rather than as the last will and testament of a doomed regime. What
really killed the liberal Republic, like its infant predecessor in 1792,
was the combined impact of military and political crisis in the
summer of 1799. The revival of the threat of invasion from outside,
combined with the eruption of renewed upheaval from within,
effectively ended any realistic hope of making the Constitution of
1795 more effective without some drastic changes. The prospects for

gradual progess simply disappeared under the pressure of events. The issue of survival inevitably took priority in these desperate circumstances. Once again the war took its toll on the course of the Revolution, driving it in an authoritarian direction, and this time it placed supreme power in the hands of a soldier.

3. Brumaire: Conspiracy and *Coup d'État*

When Sieyès began plotting the downfall of the Directory, he had little idea how he should proceed, or whom he should involve. He was spurred into action by the crisis of 1799, which confronted the Republic with the twin perils of invasion and civil war. The previous remedy for a similarly desperate situation had been the Terror, a likely outcome again on account of Jacobin ascendancy in the Legislative Councils in the spring of 1799. Yet the threat of popular dictatorship was sufficient to tip opinion in favour of the more conservative solution favoured by Sieyès. Even this experienced politician had not foreseen the reappearance of an ambitious Bonaparte, however. The unexpected return of the high-flying general from his campaign in the Middle East was the surprise element in the First Republic's last *coup*. Bonaparte's participation in the overthrow of the Directory in Brumaire produced a rather different outcome from the one envisaged by Sieyès.

1799: the embattled Republic

In the wake of the purge of parliament in Floréal VI (May 1798), both Bonaparte and Sieyès had left France, the former to embark upon his famous Egyptian campaign, the latter to become the Republic's ambassador in Berlin. While Sieyès claimed to have kept the Prussians out of subsequent hostilities, Bonaparte's adventurism undoubtedly widened the conflict. His invasion of Egypt sparked the formation of a second anti-French coalition, which now included Turkey and Russia (both alarmed by French ambitions in the eastern Mediterranean), as well as Britain, Austria, Naples and Portugal. The spectacle of Russians and Turks co-operating in the winter of 1798–9 was, in the words of Tim Blanning in his recent study of the French Revolutionary Wars, 'one of the most improbable alliances in the history of international relations'.

It was deeply ironic that Bonaparte should prove the main political beneficiary of the military disaster he had helped to unleash, though an over-confident Directory was also to blame for the ensuing *débâcle*. With Bonaparte and substantial numbers of troops isolated in Egypt, following Nelson's destruction of the French fleet in Aboukir Bay, the Republic came under severe pressure from the anti-French coalition in Europe. An early reverse in Italy was made good at the end of 1798, but in the spring and early summer of 1799 the overstretched French armies began to be pushed back along a broad Alpine front that ran from Germany, through Switzerland and down into northern Italy.

The Directory was obliged to respond to this renewed military crisis by raising more forces. French troops were thinly spread along the lengthy frontiers of the bloated Republic, and almost 50,000 of the remaining soldiers were tied up in Egypt. Even before the Second Coalition was formed, plans were being laid to replenish the ranks, and these proposals culminated in the Jourdan–Delbrel Law (named after the general and the deputy who sponsored it) which, in September 1798, introduced compulsory military service for all single men beween the ages of twenty and twenty-five. An initial levy of 200,000 men was ordered and it immediately provoked large-scale resistance, not only among the young men threatened with service on a distant frontier, but also on the part of communities loath to lose them.

Allied success in the war of the Second Coalition was thus accompanied by a resurgence of resistance in the sister republics and annexed territories, not to mention fresh upheaval within France itself. A severe clamp-down on priests and *émigrés* in the wake of the purge of right-wing deputies from parliament, in Fructidor (September 1797), had already rekindled disaffection in many areas, but conscription and associated taxation took a still greater toll on the loyalty of the long-suffering population. The Belgian departments immediately rose up in a peasant war which began in November 1798 and took two months to suppress. The conscription law was not applied in the west, where the levy of 1793 had touched off the great rebellion of the Vendée; but bands of *chouans*, who continued to ravage the countryside of Brittany and Normandy, were now joined by evaders and deserters from neighbouring departments.

As in the recent past, external defeat also served to deepen divisions within the country, reactivating both right- and left-wing extremism. The executive Directory warned against this double-headed monster in the run-up to the elections of spring 1799, but to little avail. Agents were dispatched to the provinces to engineer the victory of pro-government candidates and, if need be, to set up rival electoral assemblies at which favourable results would be guaranteed. In the event, official sponsorship was sufficient to sink many directorial nominees, while the Legislative Councils approved the elections conducted by the original assemblies in the vast majority of contested cases. A good many Jacobins were elected, while even the moderate deputies who were returned in 1799 were unsympathetic to the five-man Directory, which was blamed for the military disasters.

This general hostility to the government culminated in the so-called 'parliamentary' *coup* of 30 Prairial VII (18 June 1799). On this occasion, it was the deputies who purged the executive rather than vice versa. One Director was due for annual replacement and Reubell was selected to go. This was to deprive the five-man executive of its most capable member; worse was to follow, for Sieyès was chosen to replace him on 16 May. A Trojan Horse had been allowed to enter the government, since Sieyès was known to be a staunch proponent of constitutional change (or 'revision') as a means of escaping from the endless series of upheavals.

Sieyès has been described as 'the mole of the Revolution', on account of his subterranean role in undermining the Republic in the *coup* of Brumaire. Yet if the former churchman was the grave-digger of the Directory, he could also claim to be the midwife of the Revolution with an influential pamphlet to his credit, entitled *What is the Third Estate?*, which inspired the middle classes to take power in 1789. His most recent biographer has dubbed him 'the key to the Revolution', in the sense that he was instrumental in finding a way out of political deadlock at the start of the process in 1789, as well as in closing the door on upheaval ten years later. An intellectual rather than a man of action, who held conservative views on the nature of society, Sieyès had barely survived the Terror. Having re-emerged after the fall of Robespierre, he was profoundly alienated from the post-Thermidorian regime when his constitutional proposals found little favour among the other politicians. Every set-back for the Directory enhanced his status as an oracle and encouraged him to return to the limelight.

The destabilizing effect of Sieyès's accession to office in 1799 was soon apparent in the campaign to remove another Director, Treilhard, on the technicality that his nomination a year earlier had infringed constitutional rules; his replacement was the ineffectual Gohier. This move then paved the way to force out Lépeaux and Merlin, who were both given the choice between resignation or indictment for treason (for mismanaging the war); they opted for the former. They were replaced by two relative nonentities, General Moulin, an undistinguished soldier, and Roger Ducos, a self-effacing politician from the south-west who was a protégé of Sieyès. Of the five Directors originally elected in 1795, only the self-serving Barras now remained in post.

To describe the events of June 1799 as a victory for legislature over executive, parliament over government, would be misleading. Of course, the real triumph of Sieyès and the 'revisionists' (as those who wished to reshape the Constitution of 1795 are generally known) is more evident with the benefit of hindsight. In fact, the opposition to the overbearing and ill-judged behaviour of the Directory comprised an unstable coalition of both conservative and radical elements which would rapidly fissure once their victory over the Directors had been sealed. There was broad agreement on measures to liberate the press and secure greater freedom for voters by outlawing government interference in elections, but more drastic action to tackle the military crisis did not inspire the same unanimity. Sieyès was able to add fresh conservative recruits to his revisionist cause.

For the moment, however, it was the Jacobins who seemed to be gaining the upper hand. They fed on the crisis of summer 1799 as invasion threatened and the counter-revolution gained ever more ground. Between June and August, Russian troops under Suvorov had combined with the Austrians to drive the French right out of Switzerland and Italy. The domestic situation was also going from bad to worse. In western France several towns were briefly occupied by rebels, including Le Mans and Nantes, which were saved more by the rebels' disorganization than by determined opposition from the urban inhabitants. Unrest had also spread to the south-west, where it climaxed in an abortive royalist insurrection in the vicinity of Toulouse.

These were precisely the circumstances that had produced a whole series of draconian measures in 1793. Shades of the Terror were soon conjured up by three pieces of legislation passed in June and July 1799: an intensification of conscription, which Jourdan referred to as a new *levée en masse*; a forced loan on the rich to raise 100 million francs; and, most disturbing of all, the Law of Hostages which made relatives of *émigrés* and nobles liable to arrest and even deportation in the event of disorder in places where they resided. This set of repressive measures inevitably launched a wave of panic. Indeed, the advent of a new Terror seemed to draw still closer when, on 13 September, General Jourdan proposed that the country be declared 'in danger'.

This chilling phrase, first uttered in 1792 prior to the overthrow of the monarchy, raised the dreaded spectre of emergency government, suspension of the Constitution and popular dictatorship. Such fears were all the more potent in that government propaganda had constantly emphasized the threat of terrorism in order to safeguard the regime against a revival of the left. A recent circular from the Ministry of the Interior, for example, had summoned up the dreadful image of rough justice meted out by resurgent *sans-culottes*: 'Do you really want to see those murderers reappear, bearing bleeding heads on the end of their pikes?'

It was, however, significant that Jourdan's proposal to declare France 'in danger' was rejected in the Council of Five Hundred by 245 to 171 votes, after a tumultuous debate in which several deputies came to blows. In spite of the worsening circumstances of war and civil unrest, the Jacobin offensive had passed its peak. In July a Jacobin club had been opened in the Tuileries and numerous deputies attended its meetings, but a month later Sieyès was able to close it down with the help of Fouché, a former terrorist recently appointed as Minister of Police. Yet, while the Jacobins may have been losing momentum in the late summer of 1799, they retained sufficient credibility as public enemies for Sieyès to invoke the 'red peril' as an excuse for the *coup* in November.

Sieyès had already begun to plot his revision of the Constitution in earnest; in his view it represented the only permanent solution to recurrent crisis. The constitutional model of 1795 had already been modified when it was applied to some of the Italian sister republics that served as political laboratories for France itself: the executive had been strengthened in the Cisalpine Republic, while the Roman Constitution had established a government led by Consuls rather than Directors. Unfortunately, the legal process of constitutional revision in the French Republic was an extremely protracted one. Since Sieyès was not prepared to wait, he would obviously require military assistance to effect more immediate change by means of a *coup*. He was, however, anxious to keep the use of force to an absolute minimum and to preserve a façade of legality as far as possible. Sieyès's gaze initially fell upon General Joubert, but he undertook a fresh military command in Italy where, instead of covering himself in glory, he was killed at the Battle of Novi.

The return of the hero

Sieyès was forced to look elsewhere. His calculations were completely upset by the unforeseen return of Bonaparte, who had been extremely fortunate to evade the British fleet in the course of his escape from Egypt. After learning of the deteriorating political situation in France, together with rumours of his wife Josephine's infidelity, Napoleon decided to leave his army quite literally bogged down in the desert sands. News of recent reverses in the Middle East, whence he returned without permission, had yet to reach the French public, so Bonaparte was greeted as a hero. Any possibility that he might be arrested for desertion totally evaporated amidst the popular rejoicing that accompanied reports of his landing on the Côte d'Azur near Fréjus, on 9 October 1799. The people turned out in droves to welcome him, with cries of 'Long live Bonaparte!' and 'Long live the Republic!' resounding in the autumn air.

At nearby Toulon, the military port which had been closely associated with the naval expedition to Egypt, the town council was assembled at 4 o'clock in the morning to receive 'these happiest of tidings'. Later in the day, a celebration was held to fête 'the hero of Italy, the brave, the immortal Bonaparte', and citizens were invited to dance around a newly planted tree of liberty. Similar demonstrations of joyful relief, an indication of Napoleon's popularity, were repeated elsewhere in the department of the Var and all along the route of the general's triumphal journey to Paris. For Napoleon was anxious to head for the capital, where the Legislative Councils could hardly avoid indulging in a similar display of enthusiasm when the news reached them on 13 October. By the time he appeared before the executive Directory to report on his mission to Egypt, Bonaparte's absolution from any charge of insubordination was guaranteed.

Yet it is all too easy to present him as the long-awaited saviour, returning to lead an exhausted country that was ripe for dictatorship. Napoleon was undoubtedly popular, but he was only one of a galaxy of able, young generals currently serving the French Republic. As Michael Broers has recently put it, 'he was not untypical in an exceptional era'. Hoche, Moreau and Bernadotte were only five years older and Joubert had been his exact contemporary. Nor was his meteoric rise from relatively obscure origins especially unusual. Fellow generals had climbed the ladder of fame in record time, while political leaders of the Revolution like Danton and Robespierre had been catapulted to national prominence in a similar fashion.

Napoleon had been born into the minor nobility just thirty years earlier on the wild, beautiful Mediterranean island of Corsica. It had been ceded to France in 1768, just a year before his birth, much to the annoyance of its independent-minded inhabitants. The Buonapartes (as their family name was originally spelt – a spelling which hostile commentators would deliberately retain in order to underline Napoleon's 'foreign' origins) threw in their lot with the new masters: Napoleon was able to train as an artillery officer in the army of Louis XVI. Like many other soldiers from a relatively humble background, he owed the chance to make a name for himself to the Revolution, which threw open the ranks to men of talent and ambition. The onset of war and civil war after 1792 also provided unprecedented opportunities for advancement to those in the armed forces.

Good connections were equally essential. When Napoleon first attracted public attention and achieved promotion, after his role in ending the siege of rebel Toulon in December 1793, he was closely associated with the Jacobins. Indeed, the fall of Robespierre the following year left him politically suspect and devoid of a command. Barras, the future Director who had first encountered him at Toulon and introduced him to Josephine, rescued his military career by putting Bonaparte in charge of troops defending the National Convention against the Vendémiaire uprising in October 1795. Napoleon became a general and soon afterwards he was entrusted with the Army of Italy, not the most prestigious of appointments but one in which he made a great name for himself.

Already he was revealing political ambition and administrative skills, which probably marked him off from the other youthful generals rather more than did his military prowess. He helped to set up the Cisalpine Republic in northern Italy and negotiated the peace of Campo Formio with the Austrians. Showing a precocious flair for propaganda, he was able to glamorize his great Italian campaigns in 1796 and 1797 by means of bulletins and newspapers. The French press responded enthusiastically, awarding him the title of 'hero' for his 'Herculean exploits' in Italy and already comparing him to Caesar. In this sense, the Napoleonic legend was born on the verdant plains of Lombardy rather than on the bleak island of St Helena. He was already being proposed for a political career, though his age was a barrier to the civilian honours he had perhaps begun to covet, because the minimum age for a member of the executive Directory was forty.

The politicians in Paris were certainly discomfited by his presence when he returned to the capital from Italy in 1797. Hence their agreement to his Egyptian campaign the following year. This romantic adventure was to have disastrous consequences in diplomatic and military terms, but Bonaparte's reputation remained unscathed. He was equally untainted by political association with the discredited directorial regime, which was in such great difficulties when he unexpectedly arrived back from the Middle East in the autumn of 1799. Yet Napoleon was a general without an army, whose patron Barras was covered in ignominy. There was nothing inevitable about the acquisition of supreme power that would sharply distinguish him from a host of talented contemporaries.

The conspiracy against the Constitution

Tradition has it that Sieyès was in the process of sounding out General Moreau for the role of 'sword' or 'sabre' in his conspiracy, but having been informed of Bonaparte's reappearance, Moreau is reputed to have said: 'There is your man. He will make your *coup d'état* far better than I.' Bonaparte undoubtedly returned with burning political ambitions but, conscious of his inexperience, he was neither able nor willing to commit himself too quickly. He initially frequented the Scientific Institute, to which he had been elected in 1797 and which had supplied many of the academics who accompanied him on his expedition to Egypt, though he was also beginning to make political contacts. At his modest residence in Paris, in the side street recently renamed rue de la Victoire in his honour, he was careful to present himself out of uniform and to avoid the company of too many soldiers. He thereby enhanced his reputation as 'the most civilian of the generals'.

None the less, Bonaparte appeared to be in the process of mounting his own conspiracy, and Sieyès waited in vain for a visit from him. There was a good deal of mutual suspicion between the man of action and the man of words. The co-operation of this unlikely couple was only gradually engineered, thanks in large part to the mediation of the general's younger brother, Lucien Bonaparte, who had secured a seat in the Council of Five Hundred in 1798 as a representative for Corsica. Lucien was living down a reputation as a fiery Jacobin, and he acceded to the presidency of the chamber (which was renewed each month) on 1 Brumaire (23 October 1799), despite the fact that he was officially too young to have been elected as a deputy in the first place.

The conspiracy was rapidly becoming a family affair because Napoleon's elder brother, Joseph Bonaparte, who had made his way in directorial high society and had also become a deputy, was involved too. He wined and dined interested parties, but it was the intervention of Talleyrand, an aristocratic ex-bishop who had returned to political prominence under the Directory after falling foul of the Jacobins, that was decisive in finally bringing Sieyès and Napoleon together towards the end of October 1799. Talleyrand, memorably described by Bonaparte as 'excrement in a silk stocking', was an opportunist who had betrayed everyone yet had an uncanny knack of recognizing the winning side. He encouraged the former priest, Sieyès, and the active soldier, Bonaparte, to pool their personal ambitions; there was only room for one viable plot against the Directory.

Equally essential to the success of the projected *coup* was money, both to bribe those whose support was for sale and to pay for any associated expenses, such as printing proclamations and disseminating propaganda. The conspiracy was an expensive affair, though it is difficult to determine exactly how the necessary sums were raised since, quite understandably, the conspirators kept no detailed accounts. Sieyès and Bonaparte could draw on their personal resources, the general having amassed considerable amounts of booty during his Italian campaigns. Yet more money was urgently required, and Cambacérès, currently minister of justice, a skilful, ambitious politician with good contacts in the business world, was able to act as a go-between among the conspirators and financiers such as Récamier and Perregaux.

Army contractors, bankers and speculators were willing to dip into their own pockets to ensure that the Jacobins were brought to heel. The recent passage of the forced loan, and a proposal for monitoring the payment of lucrative government contracts that had just been endorsed by the Council of Five Hundred, were sufficient to concentrate the minds of the business community. It was no accident that the restrictions on financial settlements with contractors were thrown out by the Council of Elders on the 19 Brumaire, in the midst of the *coup d'état*, while the surtax on the wealthy was repealed less than a week after the conspirators' provisional government came into office.

There was no shortage of money or men behind the plan to overturn the Constitution. The regime was being subverted from within by its own personnel. Apart from two Directors, Sieyès and Ducos, several ministers had also been won over. In addition to Cambacérès, the ministers of the interior and foreign affairs had been suborned while Fouché, the minister of police, was ready to lend his assistance, even though some of the details of the plot were withheld from him. Leading administrators were deeply implicated, most importantly members of the departmental administration of Paris and *commissaires du directoire* posted in the capital. Numerous experienced parliamentary deputies, such as Boulay de la Meurthe and Daunou, were favourably disposed, especially in the Council of Elders, where the current chairman was an accomplice. The opposition that was anticipated in the Council of Five Hundred could be counterbalanced by the presidency of Lucien Bonaparte and a handful of his associates. Able journalists, including the former deputy Roederer, were equally committed to the plot, and there was intellectual support from the likes of Cabanis and Benjamin Constant.

Bonaparte's particular role in preparing the *coup* was to win over or neutralize various army officers. He could automatically count on a good many of his military colleagues, such as Murat who was courting and later married one of Napoleon's sisters; but other generals were more inclined to defend the republican cause. General Lefebvre, for example, who was in charge of the garrison at Paris, was loyal to the existing regime, though he was eventually prevailed upon to support the conspiracy. Bernadotte, by contrast, was sympathetic to the Jacobins and nourished political ambitions of his own; he had been minister of war in 1799, until Sieyès forced his resignation. Though he was related to the Bonaparte clan by marriage, with Joseph Bonaparte as his brother-in-law, his conduct remained in doubt until the *coup* began. He could not be persuaded to join the plot but, in the event, he did not seek to oppose it either. Generals Augereau and Jourdan, who were similarly associated with the left, likewise held aloof and were subsequently rewarded with marshals' batons.

By early November it appeared that the beleaguered regime was surmounting the crises it had faced since the summer of 1799. Masséna won a famous victory over the Russians and Austrians in

Switzerland, while Brune was forcing the evacuation of British and Russian troops from Holland. This relieved the external pressure, but the revival of French fortunes abroad was more apparent than real; the foreign threat to the regime remained dangerous and was only lifted by Bonaparte's victory at Marengo in 1800. At home, the battle for the west was far from won, and although some commentators claim that radicalism had been reduced to a mere phantom, it was a spectre that continued to haunt property-owners, especially with a further round of elections looming in the spring of 1800. In fact, the time was ripe to attempt a more permanent solution to the First Republic's continual problems of insecurity and instability. Given this uncertainty and a yearning for its resolution, the conspirators had a golden opportunity to strike and plenty of justification for doing so.

Bonaparte accordingly set the date for the *coup* as 18 Brumaire (9 November). Despite all the precautions that had been taken, the outcome was by no means a foregone conclusion. Stiff opposition could be expected from the Council of Five Hundred, where Jacobin deputies were concentrated. On account of its past history as a hotbed of unrest, there were also fears of an adverse reaction in Paris: hence the plan to remove the assemblies from the capital to Saint-Cloud, ten miles to the west, where the situation could be more easily managed, without any interference from the populace. This manœuvre, however, would prolong the proceedings and might allow the opposition to organize resistance, a development that would necessitate the very use of force that the conspirators were hoping to avoid, as they endeavoured to cloak their subversion in legality.

18 Brumaire: the constitutional coup d'état

Sieyès had begun taking riding lessons in the gardens of the Luxembourg Palace in preparation for the *coup* (much to the amusement of passers-by), but the army was intended to remain discreetly in the background. The plot was to commence by persuading members of the Legislative Councils to move to nearby Saint-Cloud, on the pretext that they were threatened by an uprising in Paris. After the assemblies had reconvened outside the capital, it would be easier to engineer the adoption of emergency measures which the conspirators were planning. This initial stage of the conspiracy was duly enacted on the morning of 18 Brumaire (9 November 1799) without much difficulty.

Just before dawn, carefully selected members of the Council of Elders were invited to an extraordinary session, which began at 7 a.m. Once they had assembled, several deputies took the rostrum in a pre-arranged manœuvre to denounce an imminent Jacobin insurrection. No real proof was supplied, but it was said that 'subversives from all over Europe had been arriving at Paris in droves during the past few days'. Then Regnier, in what the official newspaper, the *Moniteur*, misleadingly described as a 'spontaneous gesture', suggested transferring the Councils out of the capital, where they could no longer meet in safety, and putting Bonaparte in charge of all available troops. Regnier based this proposal on article 102 of the Constitution which empowered the Elders to transfer the Legislature as they saw fit, without requiring permission from either the Five Hundred or the Directory (though the appointment of Bonaparte by the Elders had no such constitutional validity). There was no debate, since up to a hundred deputies who were likely to protest had not been asked to attend the meeting. Before they dispersed, those present simply voted an address prepared by the conspirators:

> The Council of Elders invokes its constitutional authority to transfer the location of its proceedings in order to defeat the factions that wish to overthrow the national representation . . . Public safety and general prosperity, these are the objectives of this constitutional measure . . . Long live the People, by whom and in whom the Republic resides!

Bonaparte, outside whose home there had been a great deal of military activity during the early morning, was now summoned to appear before the Elders. He swore to the deputies that he and his soldiers would carry out the instructions they had been given: 'We want a republic founded upon liberty, equality, property and upon the sacred principles of national sovereignty. We will achieve our goal, you have my word!' Garat demanded that the general's oath be extended to include the Constitution, which was conspicuously absent from Bonaparte's list of objectives. The president of the Council was able to deny this request on the grounds that once the transfer of the Councils had been agreed no further discussion was permitted.

A confident Napoleon left the Tuileries to harangue his troops outside:

> In what sort of state did I leave France, and in what sort of state do I find it again? I left you peace and I find war! I left you conquests and

the enemy is crossing our frontiers. I left our arsenals full and I find not a single weapon! I left you millions from Italy and I find extortionate taxes and poverty abounding everywhere . . . The Republic has been badly governed for the past two years. You hoped that my return would put an end to all these evils, and it will; you celebrated my homecoming with a display of unity that imposes obligations upon me, which I will hasten to fulfil. It is up to you to carry out your duties and support your general with the energy, resolve and confidence that I have always admired in you. That is the way to save the Republic!

The Council of Five Hundred was assembled at 11 a.m. to hear an announcement of the transfer and, as anticipated, some deputies sought to initiate a debate. President Lucien Bonaparte responded firmly, reminding members that, according to the Constitution, all discussion was now suspended until the next day. There was considerable discontent among the deputies, who reluctantly dispersed with shouts of 'Long live the Republic! Long live the Constitution!' before drifting off to begin organizing for the morrow.

The Legislative Councils had been disposed of for the moment, but securing the compliance of the executive Directory was a little more tricky. Late in the morning of 18 Brumaire, Bonaparte prematurely announced that 'the Directory no longer exists'. To be sure, Sieyès and Ducos, the two Directors at the heart of the conspiracy, had both tendered their resignations, but Moulin and Gohier stubbornly refused to accept what was happening, while Barras was still refusing to commit himself either way. He was doubtless waiting to see how events would turn out until, presented with overwhelming evidence that the *coup* was unfolding smoothly, he was prevailed upon by Talleyrand to sign a pre-written note of resignation. [**DOCUMENT XI**] Talleyrand allegedly thanked Barras for once again 'saving the Republic', but Barras's vacillation, not to mention his unsavoury reputation, meant that there was no room for him in the new order. He would enjoy a comfortable retirement, departing on 18 Brumaire for his estate to the east of Paris. With the two remaining Directors held under guard at the Luxembourg Palace, the Directory was now indeed dissolved.

Madame de Staël, a leading literary light in the *salons* of directorial Paris, was returning to the capital that day from eastern France. She encountered Barras's coach going in the opposite direction and, having learned of events, she was surprised to find Paris so calm. Of course, a good deal of favourable propaganda had been prepared, notably by Roederer, whose reassuring *Dialogue between a member of the Council of Elders and a Member of the Council of Five Hundred* was first distributed as a pamphlet and subsequently printed in the *Moniteur*. This tract justified the transfer of the assemblies (while omitting to mention the demise of the executive Directory) and concluded that Bonaparte was neither Caesar nor Cromwell, seeking dictatorial powers; on the contrary, his presence was a guarantee that the cause of liberty would prosper. Fouché too played an important role, using his police powers to suspend the municipal administration of Paris and issuing his own placards, which were plastered on walls all over the capital: 'Let the weak take heart, they are supported by the strong. Everyone is free to go about their business and follow their daily routines in perfect confidence . . . all the necessary measures of security have been taken . . .'

19 Brumaire: a military coup d'état

Plans for the next – and decisive – day at Saint-Cloud were extremely fluid, a reflection of the conspirators' desire to proceed in a legal fashion and also their conflicting aspirations for the outcome of the *coup*. Sieyès was keen to take likely opponents into preventive custody, but Bonaparte disagreed. The former abbé was afraid that if trouble erupted in the Councils he would be unable to stop the general assuming the leading role he so obviously desired to play. This second day of the affair, which actually ran over into a third during the night of 19–20 Brumaire, is often ignored by historians. Yet the 19 Brumaire was far more critical than the more familiar 18 Brumaire, and it very nearly ended in failure. Napoleon's secretary, Bourrienne, spoke truer than he realized when, *en route* for Saint-Cloud, he crossed the Place de la Révolution, where so many fallen politicians had been executed, and suggested that the conspirators might finish up there, rather than in the Luxembourg Palace. In the event, recourse to military force was required to save the day.

Would-be opponents of the conspiracy that was now clearly unfolding may have been taken by surprise on 18 Brumaire, but they had ample opportunity to organize a riposte the next day (10 November). Indeed, because it took some time to prepare two meeting rooms for the deputies at the Château of Saint-Cloud, in the Gallery of Apollo and in the Orangery, it was the afternoon of 19 Brumaire before their sessions commenced. The Council of Five

Hundred, which opened first, set an example of resistance by demanding proof of the alleged plot that had led to the transfer. When this was not forthcoming, deputies sought to elect new directors to replace those who had resigned, and they began a roll-call affirming their support for the Constitution. This was probably a mistake, since it was a gesture of defiance of little practical value. An attempt to persuade the soldiery of what was really going on might have been more effective, though Generals Augereau and Jourdan, who were also deputies, showed no sign of wishing to seize the initiative.

The lack of progress, however, certainly unnerved Bonaparte, whose temperament and military training were ill-suited to the protracted discussions of constitutional niceties that would inevitably engage the attention of the assembled 'windbags' (as Napoleon regarded all politicians). Anxious to expedite matters, he went into the Council of Elders as soon as it had begun its proceedings and delivered a speech which left an extremely bad impression. [**DOCUMENT XII**] 'Citizen representatives', he began, 'the situation in which you find yourselves is far from normal: you are sitting on top of a volcano . . .' He continued, 'Time is short, it is essential that you act quickly. The Republic no longer has a government . . . Together let us save the cause of liberty and equality!'

Bonaparte admitted that he was 'speaking frankly as a soldier' and his military references, as well as his obvious impatience, evidently unsettled otherwise sympathetic Elders. 'What about the Constitution?' interrupted one deputy. Napoleon, who was used to giving orders and was unaccustomed to being challenged in this fashion, completely lost his composure. He responded angrily: 'The Constitution? You destroyed it yourselves. You violated it on 18 Fructidor; you violated it on 22 Floréal; you violated it on 30 Prairial. No one respects it any longer.' In response to further interventions, the general, who had reminded his listeners that his 'brave grenadiers' were surrounding the palace and that he marched 'accompanied by the god of war and the god of fortune', concluded:

> Deliberate, Citizen representatives. I have just told you some home truths that everyone has whispered to himself, but that someone must finally have the courage to say out loud. The means of saving the *patrie* are in your hands; if you hesitate to use them, if liberty perishes, you will have to answer for it before the universe, before posterity, before France and your families.

Shaken yet undeterred, Bonaparte proceeded to compound this dreadful error of judgement by marching into the Council of Five Hundred, where he was instantly greeted by cries of 'Down with the dictator!' and was prevented from speaking. Several deputies, including the heavily built Destrem, rushed towards him. In the ensuing mêlée, he was jostled and forced to leave. The famous depiction of the scene painted by Bouchot, *General Bonaparte at the Council of Five Hundred*, which now hangs in the Palace of Versailles, shows Napoleon striking a resolute pose in the midst of a group of angry, gesticulating deputies. The paintbrush, like the camera, often lies; this image is far removed from the historical reality. Bonaparte actually began to faint and had to be helped out of the Orangery by two of his trusty grenadiers.

It was his younger brother who saved the day, leading Geoffrey Ellis to comment that Lucien was 'the true hero of Brumaire'. Although he was president of the Five Hundred, Lucien was unable to maintain order. Instead, he quit the chamber and went outside to harangue the troops before they could become disaffected. He reassured them of his brother's determination to defend the sacred cause of liberty and made the dramatic gesture of putting a sword to Napoleon's breast, vowing to kill him if his words proved to be untrue.

There was no alternative now but to resort to naked force, what Thierry Lentz has called, with considerable understatement, the 'military parenthesis' in the *coup*. Napoleon ordered General Murat to clear the assembly, which was duly accomplished by troops wielding fixed bayonets. According to legend, Murat shouted to the deputies, 'Citizens, you are dissolved', followed by the rather coarser command to his soldiers, 'Throw these bastards out of here!' There was no escape for the deputies save through the windows. One officer later fondly recalled how the legislators abandoned their red togas and fine plumed hats as they fled for their lives. It was 6 p.m., and night was falling to cover the disorder and ignominy of the day in darkness.

The deputies' resistance had been admirable in the circumstances, but ultimately futile. Indeed, it was turned to the conspirators' advantage in the propaganda they subsequently issued to justify their handiwork. The uproar in the Councils could be cited as proof positive of the Jacobin plot which the conspirators claimed to have uncovered, and it also legitimized the arrest of dissident deputies. The manhandling of Bonaparte was presented in the worst possible light as an attempt to assassinate the general with a dagger. In reality the blood that ran down Napoleon's face can be explained by his nervous scratching of a spot, not by the glancing blow of a stiletto. A grenadier named Thomé was handsomely rewarded for having saved Napoleon's life by parrying another thrust, but his sleeve was more probably slit by a fellow soldier's sword than by a weapon-wielding deputy.

Once opposition in the Council of Five Hundred had been overcome, it remained to salvage some shreds of legality from the wreckage of the botched *coup* and to set up a provisional government. The Council of Elders had remained in session and many of its members were severely shaken by what had happened. When Lucien Bonaparte arrived to explain that it was Jacobin excesses that had prompted the military dissolution of the other chamber, he was badly received. None the less, the Elders set up a committee, which contained a number of conspirators, to propose the course of action that should now be taken. Despite misgivings on the part of a few members, the Elders adopted a resolution to create a temporary executive body in place of the defunct Directory, and to adjourn the Legislature for one month.

This was not enough for Napoleon, who was angry that he had not been specifically named in these arrangements. His omission probably reflected a final attempt by Sieyès to reduce the general's role in the new order. However, Lucien Bonaparte once again intervened decisively. As chairman of the dissolved Council of Five Hundred, he stood to lose all influence; hence his suggestion for reassembling as many deputies from the Five Hundred as could be found. Members of the Five Hundred would ostensibly lend greater legitimacy to the creation of a provisional government, but they could also revise the terms of a settlement in a manner more favourable to himself and his brother.

To be sure, it was only a rump of the Five Hundred that gathered at 9 o'clock on the evening of 19 Brumaire to resume its brutally interrupted session. There were just thirty deputies present, according to the historian Aulard, far too few for a quorum, but not surprisingly the official version put the total at more than 300. The survivors began by approving the military action taken against the chamber earlier in the day. Then they proceeded to establish a Provisional Consulate comprising Sieyès, Ducos and Bonaparte, in that order, which was given the task of restoring order in the country and pursuing peace negotiations with the external enemies of

France. [**DOCUMENT XIII**] The two Legislative Councils were suspended for the next three months, while two parliamentary commissions, chosen in equal numbers from each chamber, were to work at revising the Constitution. There would be a change of system, not simply a turnover of personnel.

On the advice of a small committee led by leading supporters of the conspiracy, most notably Boulay de la Meurthe, it was also decided to unseat sixty-one deputies, 'on account of the excesses for which they are well-known and not least their conduct on 19 Brumaire'. This purge followed the practice of earlier *coups*. On this occasion the overwhelming majority of those named were Jacobins from the Five Hundred, men such as Marquezy from Toulon and Briot from Besançon, who had been elected to the Legislature in 1798 or 1799. Another deputy called Aréna, who vehemently denied assaulting Bonaparte in the chamber, wrote to the left-wing *Journal des hommes libres* a few days later defiantly asserting that he considered it an honour to be included on the same list. Yet other proscribed individuals were already coming to terms with the new regime: Beyts, a deputy representing the Belgian department of the Lys, subsequently became prefect of the Loir-et-Cher; he was perhaps won over by a letter which Napoleon sent to him at the end of Brumaire. [**DOCUMENT XIV**] The outspoken General Jourdan was similarly placated and he soon resumed a military role as an army inspector.

It is instructive to contrast these 'anti-Brumairians', who initially resisted the *coup*, with fifty 'Brumairians' who were supporters of the conspiracy and were chosen to sit on the temporary legislative commissions. Most of the Brumairians were seasoned politicians who had sat in previous legislatures and seem to have despaired of bringing the Revolution to a satisfactory conclusion; Daunou was actually one of the main authors of the Constitution of 1795. These men were moderates for the most part: of fifteen former members of the National Convention, only five had voted for the king's death in 1793. If some of the men listed on the commissions were suspected of royalism, such as Arnould de la Seine who had gone into exile after the uprising of 13 Vendémiaire, others like Lucien Bonaparte can be classified as repentant radicals. The unifying characteristic of this varied group was anti-Jacobinism and a strong desire for order.

All of the Brumairians were richly rewarded by the new regime. They continued to pursue their parliamentary careers under Napoleon, and several won more glittering prizes, like Lebrun who became a Consul, and Boulay who was appointed councillor of state. Yet it would be wrong to see them merely as men on the make. In terms of their political and social outlook, they probably represented a silent majority of the deputies as a whole. At each partial renewal of the Councils, deputies solidly committed to the Constitution of the Year III had gradually been excluded. Jacobins sometimes took their seats, but former members of the Convention were more often replaced by relatively obscure men, with no previous experience of national office. In the absence of strong ideological commitment, these newcomers were anxious for stability at whatever cost.

The price to be paid for this latest 'revolution' (the term *coup d'état* was yet to enter the political vocabulary) was not immediately apparent. For when the Five Hundred concluded their shabby business in the early hours of 20 Brumaire, the Provisional Consuls dutifully swore to uphold liberty and the representative system. An executive of five men had been replaced by an executive of three (a duumvirate rather than a triumvirate, according to Vandal, for not without reason Ducos was considered a nonentity); but a new constitution was promised. There was no clear indication that this latest episode in the erratic course of the Revolution would in fact mark a watershed.

Lucien Bonaparte could not resist responding to the oath taken by the triumvirate with a typically rhetorical flourish:

> Citizen Consuls, the greatest people on earth is entrusting its destiny to you . . . Listen to the pleas of the people and its armies, who have for so long been at the mercy of the factions. Then you will earn the accolade of posterity: French freedom, which was born in the tennis court at Versailles, was consolidated in the Orangery at Saint-Cloud; the legislators of the Year VIII were the saviours of the *patrie*.

Lucien forgot to add that the deputies of 1789 had resisted the bayonets of the monarchy, while those of 1799 had succumbed to the soldiers of the Republic; the real significance of 18–19 Brumaire was yet to unfold.

Selling the coup: *lies and propaganda*

While this final charade was being played out in the legislative chambers, the conspirators were putting the final touches to the proclamations that would relay their version of events to the public and justify the measures they had adopted. Bonaparte dictated the key text that would appear on wall posters and in the *Moniteur* as an official version of these momentous events. [**DOCUMENT I**] His diatribe against the Directory and the Constitution, the condemnation of factionalism and a resolve to consolidate the Revolution, ran like a refrain through many of the declarations that followed. Napoleon made particular play of his refusal 'to be a man of party', thus placing himself high above the sordid political arena. Yet he claimed that on 19 Brumaire, instead of being welcomed in the Council of Five Hundred as a saviour, he was confronted by scenes of terror. Twenty assassins wielding firearms and stilettos were said to have thrown themselves upon him and he only narrowly escaped with his life. These anarchists had to be dispersed by force to allow the sane majority to take the necessary, salutary measures to save the *patrie*.

It should be noted that Napoleon, who styled himself as 'a soldier of liberty', made no reference to Sieyès, Ducos or his fellow conspirators in this statement, which was ominously full of the first person singular. When an initial decree from the Provisional Consulate was issued on 20 Brumaire, the names of the other consuls did appear, but Bonaparte's was to the fore, since he had presided at the new executive's inaugural meeting. [**DOCUMENT XV**] Yet, the careful presentation of the events of Brumaire to the French public was certainly a collective enterprise in which many conspirators and sympathizers took part.

Fouché, who naturally retained his post as minister of police, weighed in with a proclamation of his own on 20 Brumaire (10 November): 'The existing government was too weak to sustain the glory of the Republic against its foreign enemies and to guarantee the rights of its citizens against the factions within the country; it was, therefore, necessary to give it renewed impetus and strength.' The same day an address appeared from the officers of one of the regiments stationed in Paris, hailing the *coup* as a new start for the Republic. It was not a case of yet another faction succeeding to power; rather it signalled the death of all factions, the triumph of liberty over anarchy, of heroism over cowardice, of talent over ineptitude, and of morality over corruption. The existing Constitution was a complete shambles and a change of system was desperately required. Firm government was needed to defeat external enemies and internal rebels, and to provide liberty and equality with a more solid foundation.

As the deputy Régnault de Saint-Jean d'Angély put it, in a printed address:

> France wants something grand and lasting. Instability is fatal, it is permanence that is required. The country does not desire a royalist restoration, which has been outlawed, but it does want unity and leadership from the authority in charge of implementing the law. France wants a legislature that is free and independent, but not one that is possessed by the spirit of faction and usurpation; it wants her representatives to protect the people, not stir them up; it wants peaceful conservatives, not turbulent innovators; it wants, above all, to enjoy the fruit of ten years of sacrifice; it wants peace and liberty. Consuls, do all that is necessary to achieve these ends and your efforts will be crowned with glory!

These addresses evidently struck a chord with the public, not least in the capital, where the citizens' acquiescence was crucial to the early survival of the new regime. Yet it was hardly surprising that Paris should submit to this latest *coup*. The events of Thermidor in 1794, when Robespierre was overthrown, had marked the end of the period when decisive political events were determined on the streets of the capital by the *sans-culottes*, or in the municipal offices of the Paris Commune. The repression of subsequent political uprisings in 1795, whether led by radicals or conservatives, had left the militants with little support among the masses. Some popular support was mobilised by the Jacobins in the elections of 1798 and 1799, but otherwise power rested firmly in the hands of the directorial politicians, stiffened by the support of the generals.

What had happened at Saint-Cloud on 19 Brumaire seemed to conform to the established pattern of *coups d'état*, and it occasioned as little opposition in the capital as the purges of parliament had done in 1797 and 1798. It was still useful to play on rumours of disturbance in order to justify the measures that had been adopted, but the legendary Faubourg Saint-Antoine, the source of so many uprisings in the past, simply failed to stir. Reassured, the stock market rose several points, prompting Talleyrand to inform Bonaparte that he had made a fortune by purchasing shares on 17 Brumaire and selling them a few days later.

To be sure, ably assisted by Fouché, the conspirators took plenty of precautions to prevent any untoward reaction. The military occupied key points in the city and members of the municipal authorities, suspended on 18 Brumaire, were replaced with solid middle-class nominees. To this administrative control was added censorship of the theatre which, according to a government pronouncement on 26 Brumaire, 'had frequently resonated with gratuitous insults . . . as one party succeeded another in power'. At least three plays based on the events of Brumaire were already running and one of them, *La Journée de Saint-Cloud*, earned a particular rebuke from Fouché. The proclamation concluded that 'the current regime rejects and disdains factional disputes; it wishes to suppress them and consolidate the Republic'. In future, all new plays were to be submitted to the minister of police before they could open.

As for the press, which was represented by some seventy titles in Paris, 18 Brumaire initially prolonged a period of relative freedom. Right-wing newspapers gleefully seized the opportunity to demand persecution of the Jacobins, a monarchical restoration and freedom of worship. The left-wing *Journal des hommes libres*, which had been predicting a *coup* for several months, was understandably critical, pointing out that accounts appearing in the *Moniteur* were not to be trusted and pouring cold water on the stories of daggers allegedly wielded against Napoleon. Yet even this title stopped short of calling for outright resistance, and there was certainly no shortage of moderate papers ready to lend unequivocal support to the new regime, such as Roederer's *Journal de Paris*, and *Le Publiciste*, which was close to Talleyrand. For the latter, 'The *journée* of 18 Brumaire resembled a fête more than a revolution . . . what has occurred is not another upheaval, but the consolidation of the Republic . . . the creation of a strong and permanent political system.'

Opposition and indifference: the French people and 18 Brumaire

Too often approval of the *coup* has been taken for granted. Many historians have agreed with Mignet that 'the 18 Brumaire enjoyed immense popularity', before adding sentences such as, 'the people were waiting for a saviour to restore order. The nation was ripe for the 18 Brumaire in which it was a willing accomplice.' Yet calm in the capital ('Neither excitement nor enthusiasm', reported Fouché) should be interpreted as a sign of apathy rather than of approbation, and in the provinces, where no preparatory measures had been taken by the conspirators, the reaction was varied. The new regime inevitably inherited the disaffection that had accumulated under the Directory. There was a good deal of surprise, precious little exultation and even some opposition.

Naturally the new regime was not anxious to publicize any adverse reactions, so it is difficult to unearth many. In the departments of the Pas-de-Calais, the Yonne and the Pyrénées-Orientales the directorial authorities initially refused to publish the decree of 19 Brumaire instituting the Provisional Consulate. Similar resistance was apparently mounted at Rennes, in Brittany, but it was equally short-lived. The departmental administration in the Jura, a centre of rebellion against the Jacobins in 1793, adopted a more determined stance. Bonaparte and his colleagues were denounced as 'usurpers' and there were unsuccessful efforts to create an armed force to march to Paris and crush 'this outrage against the sovereignty of the people'.

Jacobin political clubs, which had survived in some of the larger towns, certainly protested against the *coup* and, in some cases, the military was obliged to intervene. At Versailles, local Jacobins tried to rouse the people but were frustrated by troops, while at Grenoble, where emergency measures reminiscent of the Terror had been strongly supported, General Férino closed the club to prevent further agitation. Jacobins at Toulouse offered some especially stubborn resistance. Having just overcome a counter-revolutionary uprising in the region, they were extremely critical of reactionary manœuvres in the Legislative Councils at Paris. When news of the *coup* arrived on 25 Brumaire (15 November), doubts were expressed about the justification for it, and the new executive was warned that 'the sole ambition permitted to Sieyès and Bonaparte is to save the country, not to satisfy their own egos'. However, a call to arms was stifled by General Lannes, moderate deputies from Toulouse recommended recognition of the new executive, and within a week the Jacobin club had been shut.

Partly in response to this resistance, the Provisional Consuls despatched a score of emissaries to the provinces. Following the practice of previous emergency governments, the *commissaires du consulat* were empowered to purge unreliable elements from the local administration, relying upon the support of divisional military commanders to do so. However, these roving representatives, mostly deputies from the Legislature, were sent to listen as well as to lecture. Besides disseminating the official version of events, they reported back to Paris on the current state of public opinion. Above all, their brief was 'to instruct people as to the causes of the *journées* of 18 and 19 Brumaire and to inform them of the excellent fruits they will bear'.

The speeches delivered by these *commissaires* were carefully tailored to suit the audiences they addressed. Fabre de l'Aude, for example, was sent to Provence, where he arrived towards the end of Frimaire (mid-December 1799). In the great commercial port of Marseilles, which had been devastated by the war at sea, he vigorously denounced shortcomings in the Constitution of 1795 and promised the restoration of prosperity. [**DOCUMENT XVI**] On 29 Frimaire (20 December 1799), at the nearby naval port of Toulon, Fabre served up a somewhat stronger message to a populace that had experienced great upheaval over the past ten years:

> Citizens, close your ears to the perfidious suggestions emanating from the royalist camp. There is an attempt to cast doubt upon the patriotic resolve of the new government, by insinuating that the *émigrés* will be allowed to return and that purchasers of *biens nationaux* will no longer be able to count on their acquisitions . . . Take heart, traitors and *émigrés* are banned from the Republic for ever and those who have bought national properties have nothing to fear . . .

The exiles were to be allowed home in due course but, as Fabre's address implied, in 1799 the provisional government was worried lest an essentially anti-Jacobin *coup* revived aspirations on the right. Some popular movements involving royalists occurred at Bordeaux, where the *coup* was heralded as presaging the end of the Republic and the restoration of the old Church. Right-wing youths at Nancy, in eastern France, forced the closure of the Jacobin club and draped a shroud over the door. Rumours were circulating widely about the imminent abolition of the republican calendar and the return of Sundays. According to a government official in the Mediterranean department of the Hérault, royalists had been encouraged to attack symbols of the Republic like trees of liberty and were encouraging young conscripts to abandon the colours. The royalist abbé Bernier wrote: 'It seems to me that there is a similarity between Bonaparte and Monk' (the general who had helped to reinstate the monarchy in the wake of the seventeenth-century English revolution).

Would royalists, who had not sown the seeds of the conspiracy, reap the rewards of 18 Brumaire? The prospect certainly worried Fouché, a former Jacobin who was well aware from his experience after Thermidor that repression of the left could easily redound to the advantage of the right. He was doubtless instrumental in ensuring a different outcome on this occasion. Many of the local officials purged following the *coup* of Brumaire (though we have no idea exactly how numerous they were) were removed for professing attachment to the old regime, for refusing to celebrate republican festivals, or for favouring Christian celebrations. Such insubordination was much more common than excess of republican zeal as a reason for dismissal.

This demonstration that the Provisional Consulate was implacably hostile to royalists was a good means of rallying wavering republicans. The moderate republican press in the provinces certainly endorsed the conspirators' dismal view of the Directory and expressed confidence in the revolutionary veterans who had taken the helm. Insofar as anticlericalism was a vital component of republicanism, the provisional executive's commitment to maintaining the *décadi* and prosecuting refractory priests was also warmly welcomed. Above all, there was agreement on the need for a stronger form of government to create unity and suppress the factionalism that all shades of opinion found so hard to accept as part of a liberal order. In the Burgundian department of the Côte-d'Or, the local newspaper agreed that 'our deputies were men of party rather than devoted to the public good', and its editor was greatly encouraged by the prospect of a more robust constitution to come.

The congratulatory addresses that had greeted every fresh twist in the political plot since Thermidor duly poured in from provincial France; they should not be taken too seriously nor at face value. [**DOCUMENT XVII**] Nearly all of them emanated from official bodies of one sort or another. Given the demise of clubs and societies, this should not cause any surprise, but departmental directories and municipal councils had been elected under, or were nominated by, an executive Directory in whose downfall they now rejoiced. These weary administrators frequently amended the headed notepaper on which they wrote in order to demonstrate their new allegiance to the Consulate, bending with the breeze from Paris as they had done on previous occasions. Many simply echoed the proclamations issued by the provisional government. Thus, it is not surprising to find faction and party strife vigorously condemned by many of the correspondents. Such sentiment was eloquently expressed by members of the civil court in the Saône-et-Loire:

> The Constitution of the Year III, violated and trampled under foot on several occasions, no longer offered any guarantee of security to the people; it was simply a dangerous weapon in the hands of victorious

factions, who exploited it for their own selfish purposes; we were on the edge of the abyss, when the events of 18 Brumaire occurred in the very nick of time.

Great confidence was once again expressed in the new leadership that had emerged in the capital:

> We maintained a prudent silence regarding the various journées which served to undo the Constitution of the Year III; it is not the same where the events of 18 and 19 Brumaire are concerned. The character of those who were in charge of the process holds out the prospect of a far more rosy future . . .

This was the view of one municipal council in the Rhône Valley and it was widely shared. 'The sheer joy which we experienced when we learned of the return of the great general has been far surpassed by the memorable events of 18 and 19 Brumaire', exclaimed town councillors from north-eastern France.

The tributes included some decidedly flowery – or rather fruity – language, with administrators in the Charente 'savouring the delicious fruits which the tree of liberty will bear when firmly rooted in unity, equality, security and the indivisibility of the social body . . .' Roman references naturally poured from the pens of authors educated in the classics: 'Rome owed its greatness to the creation of Consuls, and a grateful France is counting upon the same institution to restore its happiness and prosperity.' There were plenty of maritime metaphors too: 'Now that the ship of state has such experienced and talented pilots at the wheel it will surely enter the haven of stability.'

A few critical notes were occasionally struck amidst these paeans of praise. Municipal officers from Beauvais, not too distant from Paris, simply reported publishing various proclamations and concluded: 'To congratulate courageous men who risk everything for the good of their country would seem a waste of time . . .' Elsewhere optimism was tempered by caution: 'Let us hope that this new oath of allegiance to the Republic, so often sworn and so often violated, will indeed be the last.' Administrators at Ussel, in the Massif Central, added conditions to their acceptance of the *coup*: 'You will certainly deserve the blessings of the people if you prevent the triumph of reaction, restore tranquillity at home, ensure respect for persons and property, strengthen the reign of liberty and equality, destroy royalist plots and suppress all factions.' In this regard, the promised constitution was clearly crucial: 'It is for you, legislators, to give us a genuinely free constitution . . . the people desire neither anarchy nor despotism; they want a peaceful republic, freedom exercised with responsibility and respect for persons and property.'

On the assumption that documentation of this sort conserved in the National Archives offers a fairly representative sample, it is worth analysing the geographical origins of these addresses. They emanated, for the most part, from authorities concentrated in the north and east of the country. The promise of peace, both internally and externally, ensured an especially favourable response from regions like Alsace and the Île-de-France. In other words, those areas where Bonaparte would attract the most significant support in the plebiscites that followed his accession to power were already declaring their support for the new regime. On the other hand, a month after 18 Brumaire there remained twenty departments out of a hundred which had not submitted any congratulatory addresses, nearly all of them situated in peripheral areas ranging from Brittany to the Mediterranean and the south-east.

Fouché might attempt to allay the Consuls' misgivings by assuring them that the greater part of the people had endorsed the *coup*, but this was only a half-truth. There had been little overt opposition, yet apathy and resignation were the order of the day; there was little enthusiasm for what was generally regarded as an unexceptional event and scant recognition that a turning-point had been reached. If there was general agreement that 'the Revolution must be terminated, we want no more upheaval', then this consensus concealed a variety of aspirations, whether of a republican, royalist or religious nature. Much was expected from the new rulers, and the implicit suggestion behind the welter of artificial adulation was that continuing support was contingent upon a beneficial outcome, not least where a new constitution was concerned. In other words, it was a case of wait and see. The French people had been deceived too many times to put much trust in the words of the politicians. The Consulate would have to earn its keep and would only be consolidated if it kept its promises to restore peace and prosperity to a France so long deprived of both. It remained to be seen what exactly would emerge from the fog surrounding the murky events of Brumaire.

4. Despotism by Degrees: From Consulate to Empire, 1799–1804

Just as an air of inevitable failure hangs over the Directory, so in retrospect the consolidation of Napoleon's dictatorship seems to be a foregone conclusion. The reality was different. The *coup d'état* of Brumaire was merely the latest in a series of constitutional crises which had succeeded one another during the late 1790s; it was not greeted with any great enthusiasm. The conspirators were all established figures in the directorial regime and, since they claimed to be upholding the Republic, there was no immediate reason to regard this fresh twist in the plot as a major turning-point in the Revolution. Indeed, despite the promise of a new constitution, the apathy that surrounded the downfall of the Directory was deepened rather than dispelled. The new set of rulers needed to work hard to win support from a disillusioned public that had completely lost faith in its politicians; an authoritarian regime under Bonaparte would only emerge in a gradual and uncertain fashion.

Hyde de Neuville, a royalist agent stationed in Paris, was informed by one of his collaborators on 3 February 1800, almost three months after Brumaire, that 'The fall of Bonaparte appears not only certain but imminent to all those involved in the administration and the police; already a great number of his friends and acquaintances, foreseeing the decline of his authority, are distancing themselves from him.' Shortly afterwards, an anonymous pamphlet appeared, entitled *Farewell Bonaparte*. It stressed the extremely unsettled nature of the current state of affairs and likewise predicted the general's imminent downfall. In view of the rapid turnover of personalities and policies since 1789, it would have been rash indeed to predict the relative longevity of the new regime.

The foundation of the Bonapartist dictatorship was thus by no means an overnight or an assured success; it was to be a gradual and uneven process. Consolidating power was much more difficult than seizing it in the first place, and Napoleon himself had a great deal to do before he became the undisputed head of the French state. Though Ducos offered him the presidency, when the Provisional Consulate convened for the first time on 20 Brumaire (11 November 1799), 'Citizen' Bonaparte argued instead that the chair should rotate; each of the Consuls would preside in turn on a day-to-day basis.

All three Provisional Consuls were painfully aware of their temporary tenure of office in a makeshift state of affairs and, in an effort to overcome their vulnerability, they immediately passed a series of measures to shore up their shaky position. The first major decision, taken two days after their initial meeting, on 22 Brumaire (13 November), was to repeal the notorious law which allowed local administrations to take hostages from among relatives of *émigrés* and former nobles. This was a heavy-handed means of tackling counter-revolutionary disturbances which the Consuls believed was being used as a pretext for both personal vengeance and public unrest. Napoleon was reported in all the newspapers as commenting: 'It was an unjust law which deprived you of your freedom and it was my first duty to restore liberty to you.' In a typically dramatic gesture (which in today's world would have offered a splendid 'photo-opportunity'), he personally liberated several prisoners from the Temple, a former monastery which served as a prison in Paris. That same day, the Directory's 'forced loan', a progressive income tax to pay for the escalation of the war, was abolished in an attempt to mollify large property-owners, who were especially hard hit. It was decided instead to introduce an across-the-board surcharge on existing impositions.

The Provisional Consuls also nodded in the direction of greater tolerance on religious issues by cancelling deportation orders against a number of non-juring Catholic priests, while restrictions on the activities of constitutional priests, who had sworn a recent oath of loyalty to the Republic, were also relaxed. A funeral was belatedly organized for Pius VI who, as one republican newspaper report put it, had died in August having exercised 'the profession of supreme pontiff' for the past twenty-five years. This long-serving Pope became a prisoner on French soil after the revolutionary armies had occupied the Papal States and he had refused to co-operate with them. Finally, the republican festivals that had proliferated under the previous regime, partly as a substitute for the religious holidays that were banished from the new calendar, were now reduced to just two: 14 July, which celebrated the fall of the Bastille in 1789, and 10 August, commemorating the overthrow of the monarchy in 1792. The justification was that the frequency of fêtes was occasioning 'conflict between republicans'. More likely it was a recognition that official festivals were falling into disrepute and to restrict them might diminish a damaging source of friction with the religious community.

The Constitution of 1799

These placatory measures were capped by the new constitution issued on 15 December, which became known as the Constitution of the Year VIII (1799), the fourth such document that the revolutionaries had produced in less than a decade. The Brumairians were anxious to substitute a definitive regime for the provisional government established by the *coup*, just as they had promised, and they were disappointed to discover that Sieyès, the 'oracle of the Revolution', did not have a ready-made draft to hand as many of them had supposed. None the less, Sieyès advanced a number of general ideas which he had elaborated in recent years, and he exerted a decisive influence over electoral and legislative aspects of the new system. Despite his concern to strengthen the executive arm, he remained anxious to include safeguards against dictatorship, most notably by securing a division of powers. This particular principle was to be cast aside in cavalier fashion by Napoleon.

Bonaparte had little time for what he called 'metaphysical claptrap', or 'lawyers' logic-chopping', and he was keen to complete the document as quickly as possible. He was especially interested in the organization of the executive and took exception to Sieyès's proposal for a titular head of state to be called the Great Elector. This amounted to installing an elected constitutional monarch, who would nominate two Consuls, one for external affairs, the other for internal affairs, but who would otherwise occupy an essentially honorific position. The general's response to this idea was characteristically robust: 'Do you honestly think that a man of honour, a man with some knowledge of public affairs, would consent to be no more than a pig manured with millions, luxuriating in the royal palace at Versailles?'

The legislative commissions appointed after Brumaire were encouraged by Napoleon's closest collaborators to come up with a significantly modified proposal, starting with a First Consul who would serve for ten years. Even then, Bonaparte insisted that the other two members of the new consular triumvirate should have only a consultative role; he was determined to be first among unequals. Indeed, he ensured that his own nominees were placed in the subordinate consular positions. The constitutional commissions had assumed responsibility for electing the three-man executive, just as the rump of the directorial councils had chosen the provisional trio. However, Bonaparte interrupted the agreed procedure, seized the ballot papers, threw them into the fire and asked Sieyès, who was unwilling to become Bonaparte's second-in-command, to name the new triumvirate instead. Cambacérès and Lebrun were duly nominated after Napoleon.

The Second Consul, Cambacérès, was a former nobleman who became a member of the National Convention and voted for the king's death in 1793. He was an able administrator who played an important role in judicial reform under Napoleon. The Third Consul, Lebrun, was nominated for only five years (as opposed to the ten-year terms granted to his two colleagues). He had served as a royal official under the old regime, as secretary to Chancellor Maupeou (who had remodelled the *parlements*, a thorn in the flesh of the French monarchy). Like Cambacérès, he was a member of the Legislature in 1799 who supported the *coup d'état*, though his particular genius lay in the financial sphere. These two subordinate Consuls were guarantees to both left and right, though neither was drawn from the ranks of 'red bonnets or red heels' (Jacobins or royalists) whom Napoleon had vowed to exterminate. The two subordinate Consuls were, above all, competent technocrats, solid 'armrests' attached to Bonaparte's seat of power. There was no mistaking the real master: the popular answer to the question 'What is in the new constitution?' was: 'There is Bonaparte!'

Napoleon was showing his hand and, as Sieyès feared, he was emerging as the real victor among the Brumairians. Indeed, the authoritarian structure of the new regime represented something of a *coup* within the *coup* of Brumaire. The subtitle of the most recent French history of Bonaparte's advent to power deliberately employs the plural, *The Coups d'État of Napoleon*. Nor was the imposition of an overmighty executive to be the last dramatic intervention of this sort. The constitutional document of 1799 was deliberately kept short, with just ninety-five articles, as opposed to nearly 400 in its predecessor of 1795. [**DOCUMENT XVIII**] The new Constitution was 'brief and obscure', in order to leave the executive the maximum room for manœuvre. The spheres of administration and justice, which had bulked so large in previous constitutions, were organized by decree during the months that followed. Most striking of all was the omission of the Declaration of the Rights of Man and the Citizen, the 'birth certificate' of the Revolution in 1789, which had prefaced all three previous constitutions and which even today graces the title deeds of the Fifth Republic.

The vote on the Constitution

While the power of the executive was immeasurably enhanced by the Constitution of 1799, a virtually universal male suffrage was retained. All adult men, aged twenty-one years and over, who enjoyed an independent livelihood (only domestic servants were explicitly excluded, but in practice the very poor were ruled out as well), were invited to participate in a vote on the new system. In presenting the Constitution to the people on 5 Nivôse (15 December 1799), the Provisional Consuls issued a ringing declaration of intent, boldly asserting: 'Citizens! The Revolution is established upon the principles with which it began: it is over.' [**DOCUMENT XIX**]

The constitutional plebiscite or referendum (though neither term was actually employed at the time) was a device which had already been utilized twice during the preceding decade: both the Constitutions of 1793 and 1795 (though not the first attempt at a settlement for the Revolution, the Constitution of 1791) had been submitted to the electorate for approval. In both cases, the intention was to secure legitimacy for a discredited regime (notwithstanding a democratic justification for the vote) and the Consulate was seeking similar popular sanction to consolidate its precarious position. The First Consul was a strong proponent of this popular consultation, which allowed him to appeal directly to the people, over the heads of the politicians, and 'plebiscites' of this sort became part of the Bonapartist political tradition in the nineteenth century.

Significantly, the new masters of France modified the voting mechanism in an effort to obtain the overwhelmingly favourable response they so desperately desired. Instead of casting their ballots in cumbersome and potentially unruly assemblies, as voters had done for the past decade, it was decided that each male citizen should sign a register to indicate his verdict as pro or con. Many voters not only wrote down their names, but added interesting comments on the Constitution to justify the verdict they had delivered. [**DOCUMENT XX**] Only a few individuals risked identifying themselves as opponents of the emergent regime in this overt fashion. The fact that some 2,000 had the temerity or determination to do so (a few more, in fact, than the published total of 1,500 noes) is testimony to their courage, but scarcely indicative of resistance on a massive scale.

The real threat to the Provisional Consulate resided in the failure of most citizens to record a vote at all, a feature of many revolutionary elections, but not an outcome the new rulers were anxious to countenance. A poor turnout was hardly surprising since only a few days were allowed for voting, in the depths of winter. The adverse political and economic climate inevitably took a toll, and the real level of participation sometimes fell below 10 per cent in troubled areas of western France. When it became clear that most voters were abstaining, the administration simply falsified the returns to secure the desired result. This fraud, a further illegality to add to those perpetrated in Brumaire and Frimaire (November and December 1799), went undetected for the best part of two centuries. It was only in 1972 that the French historian, Claude Langlois, finally revealed the extent of the deception. The figures were rigged by Lucien Bonaparte who, as recently appointed minister of the interior, was responsible for the count. When he realized that most of the electorate were abstaining he once again intervened decisively to assist his beleaguered brother, in what Langlois calls 'the *coup d'état* of Pluviôse' (February 1800).

Surviving scraps of evidence in the archives show that officials were ordered to fabricate a higher level of participation in the constitutional referendum of 1799 than in either of its predecessors. In reality, the turnout in the Year VIII may have exceeded that recorded in 1795, but not the participation of almost two million Frenchmen in 1793. In these circumstances, totals for each department were arbitrarily inflated to produce the desired effect. Since no local breakdown of the figures was ever published, there was no opportunity for contemporaries to challenge them, though archival documentation suggests that anything up to 20,000 votes were added to each department to produce a grand total of over three million voters, roughly double the actual number of participants.

The contrived figure, which included members of the armed forces whether they had been consulted or not, represented only half of the potential electorate, but by the modest standards of the

Revolution it amounted to a massive turn-out. Above all, it allowed the regime to trumpet its superiority over previous consultations, with the confident declaration made to parliament in February 1800:

> The Constitution of the Year VIII has received over one million more votes than that of 1793, and almost two million more than that of 1795. The number of negative verdicts is far smaller than on either previous occasion. Earlier constitutions were presented to citizens at the primary assemblies . . . The Constitution of the Year VIII was submitted to dispassionate and individual reflection, in the greatest freedom and perfect security . . .

In fact, the Constitution had been put into operation on 25 December 1799 (Christmas Day was not recognized by the republican calendar) even before it had been officially approved, albeit in a fraudulent manner. This cynical 'anticipation' of a favourable outcome, which also rendered a good turn-out absolutely essential, was typical of the new regime, rendering the virtual restoration of universal manhood suffrage a sham.

According to the new constitution, all 'independent' adult males were granted the franchise and they were given responsibility for the formation of lists of their fellow citizens whom they deemed suitable to bear the burden of office, the so-called *notables*. Yet these 'lists of notability' or 'eligibility', generated at local, departmental and national levels, were obtained from a complex, indirect process and it was left to the government to decide whom they would actually appoint to office from the relevant lists. This was a screening operation far removed from democracy, even of the imperfect type that the Revolution had attempted to introduce; yet, like the 'plebiscite', it seemed to acknowledge the notion of popular consent and to preserve the sacred principle of the sovereignty of the nation.

A parliament without power

In practice only a semblance of power was entrusted to the French people, and the electoral process, which had played such havoc with the Directory, was successfully domesticated. The ranks of the *notables* were to be replenished every three years, but legislators, chosen by the government from national lists of 'candidates', were to serve for five years, and local councillors (drawn from departmental lists) still longer. These regulations ended the practice of annual elections and thereby curtailed the rapid turnover of personnel that had characterized the past decade. As Sieyès put it, the new system imposed 'authority from above', buttressed by 'confidence from below', a 'top-down' rather than the 'bottom-up' process which most revolutionaries had originally envisaged. The philosopher Cabanis, a supporter of Napoleon who was subsequently disillusioned by the increasingly authoritarian nature of the new regime, expressed the prevailing élitist sentiment quite candidly when he wrote: 'The ignorant classes no longer exercise any influence on either legislature or government . . . everything is done for the people and in the name of the people; nothing is done by them, or at their unconsidered dictation.'

The existence of two parliamentary assemblies – a Tribunate and a Legislative Body, both of which began life on 1 January 1800 – should not blind us to the reality of the new political regime. Of course, their mere existence fulfilled an important function by providing a fig-leaf of democratic respectability for the dictatorship, as well as offering a sounding-board for opinion among the *notables* (not to mention sinecures for supporters of the Brumaire *coup*). Yet neither assembly was permitted to initiate legislation, a function which belonged to the government alone. Indeed, the hundred-member Tribunate could discuss bills but could not vote on them, while the 300-member Legislative Body voted, but without any discussion (though it did receive reports delivered by deputies from the Tribunate and government officials). The parliamentary sessions were brief, though this feature clearly appealed to Bonaparte, who had told Talleyrand in 1797 how much he disliked being 'inundated with a thousand capricious laws that cancel each other out by their own absurdity'.

As Irene Collins has observed, 'The right of discussion allowed to the Tribunate was less appreciated than the silence imposed on the Legislative Body.' 'The Tribunes are getting 15,000 francs for talking – it is too much. The Legislators have 10,000 francs for keeping quiet, which is really not enough', wrote the *Ami de la paix*, one of the few surviving newspapers. None the less, the old habits of parliamentary opposition were not entirely effaced and, for the moment at least, they had to be tolerated. Benjamin Constant, for example, used one of the first sessions of the newly created Tribunate to proclaim the assembly's independence and authority, without which, he contended, 'There is nothing but servitude and silence – a silence that the whole of Europe will hear.' Such dissent was subsequently overcome by purging the Tribunate's membership and trimming its powers; later on, in 1807, this arm of the legislature was finally amputated.

Sieyès appears to have realized at least one of his long-cherished ambitions in the Constitution of 1799: the creation of a constitutional court. This body was to determine the constitutionality of legislation and serve as a workshop for constitutional amendments, as well as choosing members of the Legislature. In fact, the Senate, as it was called, soon lost control of nominations to parliament, while *senatus consulta* (effectively 'informing the Senate') became a means for Bonaparte to rule by decree. The Senate helped to adapt rather than to preserve the Constitution, offering little resistance to the further growth of Napoleon's powers in 1802 and 1804. Sieyès consoled himself with the presidency of the Senate (where the other former Provisional Consul, Ducos, found a refuge as his deputy) and was allowed to nominate his friends as richly remunerated senators. In effect, Sieyès himself became the 'pig manured with millions' whom Bonaparte had stridently denounced during earlier debate on the Constitution. Not only was the former *abbé* endowed with substantial wealth; the most famous opponent of the aristocracy in 1789 ended up in 1808 as a member of the imperial nobility.

One key to the gradual consolidation of the new regime was its ability to win over many politicians who had not been numbered among the Brumairians and who, in some cases, had opposed the *coup d'état*. Having taken the sting out of elections and representative institutions, Bonaparte was able to persuade republican antagonists to sink their differences in his lucrative service. This policy of reconciliation is immediately apparent in the personnel of the Senate and the two parliamentary bodies, since the great majority of their members had occupied legislative office under the Directory and espoused a variety of political viewpoints. Such a high degree of continuity with the personnel of the preceding regime was a bitter disappointment to sections of the press, which felt that the new rulers were failing to honour their promise to save France from the self-seeking factions of the past. The *Diplomate* ridiculed the familiar names crowding the Tribunate and the Legislative Body, parodying the Catholic creed with the words: 'From the eternal politicians, deliver us, O Lord!' There were, however, limits to the *ralliement* at this stage: few regicides were to be found among these recruits to the Consulate, while declared royalists also remained beyond the pale.

The administrative state

Sympathetic journalists need not have worried too much about the new regime's apparent endorsement of long-serving politicians; real power resided elsewhere. The new order reasserted executive authority, which had so often been overruled by the Legislature during the past ten years. At the very heart of the emergent Bonapartist system was the Council of State. Together with Bonaparte himself, this hand-picked body of experts, which originally comprised twenty-nine individuals from a variety of political and social backgrounds, became the effective legislator of France. Besides advising Bonaparte on a wide range of administrative matters, these councillors initiated all the legislation submitted to parliament which, in the event of opposition, was easily circumvented by means of the *senatus consultum*. The work of the Council was conducted *in camera* and it was at this level of the apparatus alone, where policy was originated and elaborated, that Bonaparte was prepared to countenance genuine debate and disagreement.

Ministries, by contrast, were of rather less importance, and ministers were deprived of any real latitude in the exercise of their duties, implementing rather than formulating policy. Even so, a huge array of activities, from agriculture to education, depended upon the Ministry of the Interior, the major authority, which was briefly occupied by Lucien Bonaparte and then by the able and energetic, former academic Chaptal. The massive correspondence generated by the Interior Ministry amply justified the credo of Montalivet, a later incumbent: 'The centre must know whatever is being done, for good or ill . . . We must have analyses that show what is being done or not done, in different places and at different times.' The dictatorship at Paris was in vain if decisions were not executed in the localities.

Non-compliance at the grassroots level had been the bane of government for much of the 1790s. To be sure, the Directory was far less decentralized and liberal than is often supposed. The presence of central agents in the provinces was built into its structure, and it can be argued that the *commissaire central*, attached to each department after 1795, was in some respects a forerunner of the Napoleonic prefect, who became the key figure in local administration. Bonaparte had firm foundations on which to build in the provinces and, contrary to popular misconception, he did not create the departments into which present-day France is still divided. On the eve of Brumaire there were already just over a hundred of them in existence (see map 2 on p. xii). The original eighty-three departments carved out in 1790 had grown as the territory of the Republic expanded after 1792, and their number would continue to rise as further areas were annexed to France.

While Bonaparte did not invent the departments, he profoundly altered the way in which they were run, by means of the changes enshrined in the administrative law of 28 Pluviôse VIII (17 February 1800). The prefects installed at the head of each department were given extensive powers and still greater responsibilities. [DOCUMENT XXI] They could issue local decrees and they appointed mayors in the smaller communities. Yet, like their assistants, the sub-prefects, who were placed in charge of the *arrondissements* into which the departments were now subdivided, prefects were hired and fired exclusively by the First Consul. Bonaparte might tell Castellane, prefect of the distant Basses-Pyrénées, situated on the border with Spain, that he could behave like 'a pasha' in his far-flung domain, yet the prefects were agents rather than associates of the central power, assuring the execution of orders and the regular transmission of information.

The First Consul himself named mayors in the larger towns of over 5,000 inhabitants, and he also nominated members of the various councils which continued to exist at departmental, *arrondissement* and municipal level. Such bodies had effectively controlled local government during the preceding decade, but in future they would only meet infrequently and generally conduct their business in a docile fashion. Their task was reduced to rubber-stamping the decisions of permanent officials who were appointed to implement central policy, a far cry from the often anarchic, local initiatives of the revolutionary period.

The Bonapartist system proved extremely effective and underwent few substantial modifications until the late twentieth century, but it was no overnight success. It functioned imperfectly at the outset since stability of personnel took some time to achieve; roughly half of the first cohort of prefects were replaced within two years. Once again, the Bonapartist regime was able to draw on a broad range of talents, largely ignoring previous political allegiances and ranging from monarchists like Mounier, appointed to the Ille-et-Vilaine in Brittany, to regicides like Thibaudeau, who was briefly dispatched to the Gironde. Most of the first generation of prefects had acquired some administrative experience at departmental level during the

Revolution. It was above all for their competence as 'technocrats' that they were chosen, like other leading servants of the regime.

The same centralizing and authoritarian spirit informed the reorganization of the judicial system, according to the law of 18 March 1800. This retained the hierarchy of courts established during the Revolution, but it suppressed the election of judges, who were now appointed for life by the First Consul. The justices of the peace, who arbitrated petty disputes in the localities, were still to be elected. The new regime initially hesitated to meddle with a revolutionary innovation that had proved so popular with the people. Yet from 1802 onwards the voters lost their direct control over these JPs; in future their role was restricted to the presentation of two 'candidates' to the First Consul, who made the final choice. Juries were also retained, despite Bonaparte's misgivings, but special courts were employed without juries when the interests of the state were deemed to be at stake. Most famously, Napoleon hastened completion of a whole series of legal codes, chiefly the Civil Code (or Code Napoléon) of 1804, which created a uniform system for the whole of France. There was a clear framework for the rule of law, even though the sovereignty of the people had become an empty shell and citizens had been transformed into little more than *administrés* by Bonaparte's bureaucratic reforms.

The appointment of personnel to fill posts in the radically reshaped administrative and judicial system inevitably took some time to achieve. In the short term, the replacement of officials elected under the Directory often disrupted rather than smoothed the governmental process. Moreover, an element of passive resistance to the new regime is indicated by the unwillingness of numerous nominees to serve the consular government, at the local level in particular. For example, at Toulon, the turbulent Mediterranean naval town, three municipal officers refused to serve under the newly nominated mayor, a former nobleman whom they deemed to be a royalist. The prefect of the Var, who was struggling with similar problems elsewhere in this volatile southern department, warned the government that replacements would be hard to find. At Toulon, he wrote, 'You will find few men renowned for their love of liberty who wish to work with the new mayor', and it took more than three months to arrive at a compromise. A year later, however, he was able to sound a more optimistic note, suggesting that the return of stability was slowly encouraging opponents to make their peace with the new order.

The role of repression

This nascent administrative state, which effectively negated the electoral principle while retaining elections of sorts for a much-reduced number of posts, inevitably restricted the liberties of the individual. Liberty had been the first and greatest in the celebrated revolutionary trinity of Liberty, Equality and Fraternity, but now it was relegated to last place in the official slogan which Bonaparte concocted: Property, Equality and Liberty. Critical publications continued to appear, and freedom of the press was an early casualty of the consular regime. This is not to say that restrictions had not been imposed during the preceding decade, but the decree of 17 January 1800 was especially draconian and it was not subsequently reversed. On the pretext that national security was at risk in time of war, the seventy-three titles published in Paris were reduced to just thirteen. [**DOCUMENT XXII**] Surviving editors were subjected to constant harassment as Napoleon, who had fully grasped the importance of propaganda and censorship, sought to manipulate the press to his own ends.

Bonaparte might seek to woo and reconcile, but he was never afraid to strike hard at residual opposition. This side of the Consulate is reflected in the growth of the police force, which was essentially the responsibility of the former terrorist Fouché, but it was most clearly apparent in the use of special courts to try particular categories of offenders. Once again the Directory had sown the seeds of such policies, though the Consulate reaped a more repressive harvest. Military tribunals were used not only to try political opponents, but also to deal with violent criminals and bring them swiftly to justice. It was certainly difficult to say where brigandage pure and simple ended and politically motivated activities began. Bands of draft-dodgers and deserters from the army, for example, often masqueraded as royalists to justify their lawlessness. At all events, what Howard Brown calls the 'security state' rapidly evolved with the increasing use of this draconian form of justice against both crime and dissent.

Bonaparte's first year in office was extremely troubled as a result of the military crisis of 1799. On the one hand, resistance to conscription and taxation spawned more rebels, while, on the other, the diversion of the army to the frontiers left fewer soldiers to police the interior of France. In an effort to distance the Consulate from the Directory, emergency measures like the notorious law of hostages were immediately repealed, but the persistence of unrest that the new regime inherited meant that the rule of law could not be upheld without resorting to similar means of repression. Indeed, at precisely the same moment that the hostage law was being repealed, the law of 9 January 1798, which authorized the trial of civilian offenders in military courts, was reintroduced by the Provisional Consulate as a vital weapon in the war on brigandage.

Bonaparte's claim in November 1800, on the first anniversary of his accession to power, that he had restored order 'without shedding a single drop of blood' was therefore disingenuous, not to say a downright lie. Besides making the well-publicized gesture on the hostage law, he had ostentatiously commuted Sieyès's deportation of Jacobin opponents to house arrest. The *coup* of 18 Brumaire was not accompanied by the murders or executions that had marked other *journées* in the Revolution, such as 10 August 1792 or 9 Thermidor 1794. Yet in Brittany, for example, the new Constitution was quickly suspended, and General Brune relied heavily upon the military courts in his efforts to crush the *chouans*.

Even after victories on the battlefield had facilitated the return of troops from Italy in the summer of 1800, the internal situation remained anarchic in many areas. As a consequence, during the winter of 1800–1, flying columns of soldiers and local militia were ordered to employ a shoot-to-kill policy against armed brigands, while additional military commissions were established to try those taken alive. Two commissions operating in Provence and Lower Languedoc judged 461 men and women, of whom 266 were put to death after conviction, a total which does not include several dozen killed in the fighting or attempting to escape. When such measures proved rather too arbitrary, Special Tribunals were created by the law of 7 February 1801, and they were subsequently set up in no fewer than twenty-six troubled departments in western and southern France. [**DOCUMENT XXIII**] Prisoners were brought to trial within three days of arrest, judgements were delivered without juries, and there was no right of appeal. The offences over which these courts had jurisdiction were very wide in scope, ranging from vagrancy to burglary, and from murder to sedition. Moreover, the Special Tribunals remained a permanent feature of the Napoleonic judicial system, though their use seems to have diminished as this repressive regime began to wear down even the most determined resistance.

The vigorous pursuit of law and order gradually facilitated the extension of the Consulate's authority and vice versa. Although it is necessary to dwell on those repressive aspects of the new regime that are now coming to light, this severity was certainly accompanied by a series of conciliatory measures which pacified many former opponents of the Republic. Relaxation of the laws against *émigrés* was among the most important of these placatory policies. The closure of the official lists of political exiles on 12 Ventôse VIII (3 March 1800), which implicitly curtailed the prohibition on leaving the country without permission, encouraged the wholesale return of hundreds of *émigrés*. It was followed by a general amnesty two years later, which excluded from repatriation only 1,000 of the most notorious exiles who continued to work for the royalist cause. The process of reinstating these returnees to full citizenship would be a lengthy one (and there was no restitution of property confiscated from *émigrés* by the government), but Bonaparte was thereby healing some of the deepest wounds caused by the revolutionary upheaval.

Compromise with the Church

None of the injuries inflicted by the Revolution on the body politic of France was more traumatic than the religious strife. The outstanding feature of the conciliatory side of the Consulate was the settlement with the Church, which disarmed the royalist opposition far more effectively than repression alone. Constitutional and refractory clergy remained at odds, despite attempts to reunite them, while organized religion was at the mercy of a republican government committed to the promotion of secular culture and at best completely indifferent to Christianity. Only a restoration of the monarchy, it seemed, could end both religious schism and division.

Bonaparte took a typically pragmatic – not to say cynical – view: 'no church, no government', he wrote to his brother Lucien in 1801. The Provisional Consulate had made some initial gestures of religious appeasement, a trend continued under the Consulate proper, though it was necessary to tread warily in this veritable minefield. Fouché, who as minister of police was responsible for overseeing the clergy, was deeply concerned that any relaxation of the controls on worship would encourage a religious revival and under-mine the ten-day week. Bonaparte, by contrast, was convinced that the promise of greater religious latitude had helped to pacify rebellion in western France and that such a policy would yield massive rewards elsewhere in the Republic.

By chance, the cardinals of the beleaguered Roman Catholic Church were meeting in conclave at Venice to choose a new Pope just as Bonaparte was coming to power in the *coup* of Brumaire. Pius VII, the newly elected pontiff, proved to be as anxious to arrive at a compromise as was Napoleon, since he was well aware of the damage that the continuing schism in France was causing. He was consequently willing to abandon both the Bourbons and the French bishops as the price of a religious settlement. Bonaparte was quick to seize the opportunity to strike a deal. As he put it, employing characteristically military terminology, the Pope has forces equivalent to 'a corps of 200,000 men'. Whereas the Papacy had been completely ignored when the French Church was reformed early in the Revolution, the ecclesiastical restoration under the Consulate ten years later was transacted exclusively with the Pope, over the heads of constitutional and refractory clergy alike.

Some extremely tough and protracted negotiations ensued, with particular dispute arising over the status of Catholicism in the Republic. This was simply described in the final version of the Concordat that emerged as 'the religion of the great majority of French citizens', not as the religion of state, as the Pope preferred. [**DOCUMENT XXIV**] There was no question of abandoning religious toleration (one of the gains of the Revolution); Protestants and Jews came to separate agreements with Bonaparte. Equally fundamental was the renunciation by the French Church of its pre-revolutionary property holdings: 'His Holiness . . . declares that neither he nor his successors will in any way disturb the purchasers of alienated ecclesiastical property . . .' This was an essential guarantee for countless property-owners who had profited from the massive transfer of Church lands to private ownership during the Revolution.

Since Napoleon agreed to remunerate the clergy, he was granted the right to nominate bishops, and also the power of veto over the choice of parish priests. This authority was immediately employed, for all incumbents were obliged to resign their offices when the Concordat came into effect. The French clergy as a whole protested, but the biggest losers from the resulting turnover of ecclesiastical personnel were in fact the constitutional clergy, few of whom were awarded places on the new bishops' bench. The abbé Grégoire, a leading constitutional bishop who had tried so hard to integrate Church and Revolution, was a prominent victim of the bargain which Pius VII and Napoleon struck. Anticlericals were equally dismayed, though Bonaparte tried to reassure them by unilaterally appending the Gallican articles to the remarkably brief Concordat. These provisions, which regulated supposedly administrative matters such as festivals and processions, but also further reduced the number of dioceses, were added after the main document had been ratified. The Pope was bitterly disappointed by Bonaparte's deception, but he decided that no price was too high to secure the restoration of regular worship in the French Republic.

The Roman Catholic Church in France was literally resurrected when the Concordat came into effect on Easter Sunday, 18 April 1802 (though officially, and somewhat incongruously, the revolutionary calendar remained in being for the next four years). The occasion was celebrated at the great cathedral of Notre-Dame in Paris with suitable pomp and splendour. A few generals muttered their disaffection and railed against the re-emergence of a 'superstition' they had fought to destroy; according to one of them, the only absentees from the ceremony were 'the thousands who had given their lives in the fight against fanaticism'.

The restoration of the Church seems to have been popular in most parts of France, and it was especially welcome in the annexed departments of Belgium and the Rhineland. Some returning priests created local difficulties by refusing the sacraments to those who had sympathized with the Revolution, while many clergy remained monarchist at heart. [**DOCUMENT XXV**] Nevertheless, the religious settlement removed a potent weapon from the royalists' arsenal and bolstered the regime with a spiritual blessing. An oath of allegiance to the Republic was taken by all priests, while prayers were offered and thanks rendered for its rulers. Prelates became popularly known as 'prefects in purple' and parish priests as 'mayors in black'; they wore a different costume from their secular counterparts, but performed a similar supporting role.

From victory to peace

It is significant that publication of the Concordat was deliberately delayed until the declaration of peace in 1802, when first Austria and then finally Britain came to terms with the Consulate. Although the military crisis caused by the victories of the Second Coalition had been alleviated before Napoleon came to power in Brumaire, the situation remained acute. The new regime desperately needed to consolidate its position outside the country as well as within. As head of the army, as well as head of state, the First Consul was personally in charge of French forces, though this responsibility left him exposed to the fortunes of war. In the spring of 1800 General Bonaparte accordingly set out to cross the Alps and take his Austrian enemies by surprise on the plain of Lombardy. This daring and dramatic strategy recalled the exploits of Hannibal and was immortalized on canvas, but it nearly came to grief.

The fate of the Consulate and perhaps of Europe was decided on 14 June 1800 on the battlefield of Marengo, just outside Alessandria. Napoleon committed a tactical error by dispersing his troops and ended up facing the entire Austrian army with reduced numbers. The French were losing the fight when the arrival of General Desaix, who was destined to die in this bloody battle, turned the tide. Napoleon immediately issued a misleading bulletin presenting another irresistible victory inspired by his charisma. [**DOCUMENT XXVI**] In fact, the hapless Desaix, who never uttered the dying words attributed to him (but Bonaparte was not inclined to allow the truth to spoil a dramatic story), had saved his master's political skin; a decisive defeat might well have destroyed the incipient dictatorship. The politicians had been plotting to replace the general since his departure from Paris. In the opinion of François Furet, when Napoleon returned triumphantly to the capital in July, amid much popular rejoicing, he must have realized that 'Marengo, far more than Brumaire, was the true coronation of his power.'

The victory of June 1800 paved the way for peace with the Austrians at Lunéville in the following February, when the Habsburgs ceded all territory on the left bank of the River Rhine to France. Only the British remained at war, supreme at sea but bereft of a continental bridgehead since their ejection from Portugal. Terms which recognized French domination of western and southern Europe were hammered out with Britain during the autumn of 1801 and eventually signed on 27 March 1802 at Amiens (the town in north-eastern France from which the treaty took its name). Bonaparte could now present himself as both conqueror and peacemaker, to decisive political effect at home. More significant in the long run, however, was the inextricable link he had forged between success on the battlefield and the future of his regime. News of the initial reverse preceded that of the ultimate victory at Marengo and, for a few hours, there was intense speculation in the capital as to who should succeed the hero. The underlying, ultimately fatal, fragility of the Bonapartist regime was thereby revealed.

The Life Consulate

As the Consulate grew in stature, so important modifications to its political structure were made. General Bonaparte was obviously no General Washington, the military hero of the American Revolution who served as president of the Republic and then retired on the expiry of his four-year mandate. Bonaparte was not seeking to consolidate the Republic simply to hand it over to someone else. Indeed, shortly after delivering a eulogy to Washington, who died in December 1799, Napoleon decided to separate himself from his fellow Consuls and took up residence in the Tuileries, the former palace of the kings of France. Yet royalists were deceived if they drew any encouragement from the move, for it was unlikely that Bonaparte would play the same role for the exiled Louis XVIII that General Monk had filled for Charles II at the end of the republican experiment in seventeenth-century England. The pretender to the French throne lost no time in sounding out Bonaparte, who waited to reply until after his victory at Marengo. Then, in August 1800, he famously counselled the would-be king:

> You should not seek to return to France; you would have to walk over one hundred thousand corpses. Sacrifice your interests for the sake of France's peace and happiness. History will take account of your action . . . I am not, however, insensitive to your family misfortunes. I will contribute with pleasure to the pleasantness of your retirement.

Although he was eligible to serve for a second term, the ten years for which Bonaparte had been appointed First Consul soon began to seem rather short, especially in view of his relative youth. There was continuing concern about the future, since any hereditary succession was ruled out by the current constitution, not to mention the First Consul's lack of an heir. Josephine was unable to provide her husband with a child, though she did have a son and daughter by her previous marriage. Lucien Bonaparte suggested she 'take the waters', in other words contemplate a health cure in order to improve her child-bearing prospects. If, and until she did so, speculation regarding the long-term viability of the regime would only intensify.

Uncertainties such as these led to the creation of the Life Consulate in 1802 and the provision that Bonaparte should nominate his own successor. These changes were, of course, thoroughly contrived, and involved some adroit manœuvring in order to secure the desired end. It had been agreed in advance that the Tribunate should invite the Senate to 'offer the Consuls a recognition of the nation's gratitude' for the respite from war secured by the Treaty of Amiens. The proposal was duly made on 5 May 1802, but senators mistakenly thought that Bonaparte would be satisfied with a further term of ten years as Consul; he was not. On the pretext that only the people could decide the matter, the Council of State intervened with the announcement of a referendum, which asked the people to pronounce on the following question: 'Should Napoleon Bonaparte become Consul for Life?'

This consultation took place at the end of May 1802 under similar conditions to the previous 'plebiscite', held immediately after Bonaparte came to power. The issue on this occasion was more straightforward; instead of being asked to cast their votes on a constitution, all adult males were simply invited to record an opinion for or against a short proposition creating the Life Consulship. Registers were opened in local administrative offices for up to three weeks to receive a verdict. This offered a longer period in which to vote than the time made available two years earlier, and many more citizens participated than before. There is less reason to dispute the official figures released in 1802, for they were published in full and suggested that three and a half million civilians and soldiers had voted in favour of the Life Consulate. The north and west of France was rather less enthusiastic than the south and east, but it was rare for the turnout anywhere to fall below the level of 25 per cent.

The bulk of some 8,000 negative verdicts cast in 1802 emanated from the armed forces, where revolutionary sentiment remained deeply entrenched and there was a surprising willingness to demonstrate it. Relatively few misgivings were expressed by civilians. There was undoubtedly organized administrative pressure to participate, which had certainly not been the case two years earlier: the prefect of the Cantal, for example, urged citizens to support the hero who had achieved such wonders as peace in their time and a religious restoration, warning that without him disorder and faction would again flourish. Mayors acted in a similar fashion in the villages, taking groups of citizens along to vote and signing the register on their behalf if they were unable to do so themselves. Some of the departmental returns seem to be implausibly high, well above the average turnout of approximately 50 per cent. Yet, when all is said and done, roughly twice as many civilians appear to have voted in 1802 as at the end of 1799, a convincing testimony to the consolidation of the consular regime.

It was, of course, typical that even before the votes were counted, the government should decide to elaborate upon the simple proposition inscribed in the plebiscite. The republican historian Aulard has accordingly slated the Life Consulate as yet another Bonapartist *coup d'état*. In the words of Napoleon himself, 'The Senate desired what the French people wanted . . .' **[DOCUMENT XXVII]** The decree of 4 August 1802 on the Life Consulate actually amounted to a fresh political settlement, which has become known as the Constitution of the Year X (1802). It was slightly shorter than its immediate predecessor and once more it excluded any declaration of rights. It began by profoundly modifying the electoral system. The lists of *notables*, which Bonaparte had never liked, were abolished and restrictions on eligibility to office were reintroduced instead. In future, members of the departmental electoral colleges would be chosen from among the 600 highest taxpayers. This represented an important statement concerning the designated social basis of the regime; Napoleon referred to the *notables* as 'blocks of granite' on which he wanted to build the new order. Yet, since the assemblies would meet only rarely and were limited to the presentation of candidates for office, the net result was to tighten the government's grip on the choice of parliamentary personnel and local councillors.

Indeed, the powers of the Legislature were substantially reduced and, together with subsequent modifications passed by decree, the power of the First Consul was immeasurably enhanced. He was now able to dissolve parliament, for example, and he was no longer obliged to refer alliances or peace treaties to the deputies for ratification. Above all, as well as becoming Consul for as long as he lived, Bonaparte was entitled to name his own successor, albeit subject to posthumous approval by the Senate. A kind of republican monarchy was thus in the making, an impression confirmed by the bloated civil list that increased the resources at Bonaparte's personal disposal to six million francs per annum. The First Consul himself was extremely abstemious, eating frugally and dressing simply (even shabbily, according to visitors), but this huge sum enabled him to begin creating a court at the Tuileries. It was at this point that his effigy began to appear on the coinage, after the manner of former kings. As the historian Jacques Godechot suggests, Napoleon had not simply surpassed the constitutional authority that Louis XVI was given during the Revolution; he was already beginning to rival the absolutism of Louis XIV.

Towards the Empire

Yet consolidation of the Consulate within France was not matched by a lasting settlement in Europe. The Peace of Amiens was no more than a brief truce separating two decades of continuous international conflict. The short-lived treaty was broken by violations which occurred in virtually every sector that it covered, from the Low Countries to the Mediterranean. On 12 May 1803 Britain recalled its ambassador from Paris. A third anti-French coalition was under construction and hostilities soon recommenced. This resumption of war had a crucial bearing on the constitutional situation in France because it revived fears concerning the succession to Bonaparte. The solution was to pursue the logic of the Life Consulate to a hereditary conclusion in the creation of the Napoleonic Empire.

Another plot to assassinate Napoleon was being hatched at precisely this juncture. It was by no means the first such attempt: on 3 Nivôse IX (24 December 1800) a gunpowder bomb, the so-called *machine infernale*, exploded in Paris as Napoleon made his way to the Opera. Over a hundred Jacobins were deported as a consequence, though the police chief Fouché was well aware that royalists were responsible (there are suspicions that other alleged 'plots' were mounted by the authorities to justify repression). However, with British assistance, right-wing opponents of the consular regime certainly did continue to target Napoleon. In 1803 Georges Cadoudal, an inveterate counter-revolutionary who had fought in the Vendée and then participated in *chouannerie*, crossed the Channel with the express aim of assassinating the First Consul. General Moreau, an ambivalent associate of Bonaparte, was informed of the conspiracy but he neither joined nor divulged it. The game was actually given away by an informer and, in the spring of 1804, all those involved were rounded up and incarcerated. Moreau was subsequently exiled, while Cadoudal and other conspirators were executed.

The signal for the assassination was apparently to have been the arrival of a member of the royal family on French soil. Fouché accordingly informed Bonaparte of the presence in Baden, just on the other side of the Rhine frontier, of the duc d'Enghien, a relative of Louis XVIII. He was kidnapped, brought to France, tried and shot at dawn on 21 March 1804. Was this a heinous crime or an act of public safety? Bonaparte willingly accepted responsibility and, whatever his real motives, the outcome of this 'regicide' was clear: it ended any lingering hopes of a deal between the First Consul and the pretender to the Bourbon throne, and it also prepared the French people for the establishment of the First Empire.

This was a somewhat curious development insofar as Bonaparte lacked a legitimate heir (only later would he obtain one, after he jettisoned Josephine and married the Habsburg princess, Marie-Louise). Napoleon's personal preference for his younger brother Louis as a successor also provoked bitter animosity within the Bonaparte family. Above all, although the Republic had become something of an empty shell with the adoption of the Life Consulate, the formal adoption of a monarchical system, albeit in the absence of the legitimate king, distanced the Bonapartist regime still further from the Revolution. A number of prominent politicians were strongly opposed to this retrograde step towards the old regime, most notably Carnot, the famous 'organizer of victory' in 1793. Resistance in the army, which remained a bastion of republican sentiment, was especially widespread.

None the less, the matter was pressed forward according to Bonaparte's wishes and the Tribunate spontaneously 'requested', as planned, that the title 'Hereditary Emperor of the French' be conferred on him. In a final, if spurious, homage to the democratic principle, the proposition was put to the people in a third plebiscite. Once again, the results are not easy to interpret, given the unanimous verdict recorded by the armed forces, the implausibility of some returns indicating a turn-out of over 100 per cent, and the administrative pressures that were evidently employed. The prefect of the Norman department of the Eure, for example, gave the game away when he suggested that turn-out was rather unpredictable, not because of variations in public opinion but as a consequence of different degrees of activity on the part of local mayors.

The administration was obviously determined to present a higher vote in 1804 than in 1802, and duly produced a total for the Empire that surpassed the figure for the Life Consulate: in excess of three and a half million votes were allegedly cast in favour of Napoleon's imperial pretensions. There is, however, incontrovertible evidence in 1804 of the falsification of returns in the Ille-et-Vilaine and the Loire-Inférieure, in western France. Allowance also needs to be made for additional departments included in this count, as French authority continued to extend into Europe. It is quite clear that *fewer* civilians voted in 1804 than in 1802; indeed, a decline of at least 15 per cent was evident. Departments along the eastern frontier continued to turn out strongly, but Napoleon was losing many supporters in the southern half of France.

The outcome of this latest referendum would suggest a cooling of enthusiasm for the Bonapartist regime, perhaps as a result of misgivings over the resumption of war. Yet the degree of support expressed in this third consultation was still a solid one. The sycophantic responses from former republicans, who described themselves as 'humble servants' and addressed Napoleon as 'Sire', certainly stick in the throat. The letter from the Brumairian Sédillez is especially nauseating: 'I voted for you on 19 Brumaire, I voted for the Constitution of the Year VIII, I voted the same way on the Life Consulate, because a vote for you is a vote for the salvation of France.' Not all voters were similarly obsequious; others indicated their sincere endorsement of a successful regime and their desire to see it perpetuated in a different format.

A further modification of political institutions, the so-called Constitution of the Year XII (1804), accompanied the proclamation of the First French Empire on 18 May. [**DOCUMENT XXVIII**] Once again a Senate decree was employed to effect this final step in the evolution of the Bonapartist dictatorship. The succession required definition, as did a series of imperial dignitaries; most importantly, the role of parliament was circumscribed to a still greater extent as Napoleon tightened his authoritarian grip on post-revolutionary France.

All these aspects of the Empire were quite literally crowned in the elaborate ceremony staged at the cathedral of Notre-Dame on 11 Frimaire XIII (2 December 1804), a noteworthy date in the Bonapartist calendar since the famous victory at Austerlitz occurred exactly one year later. The coronation of Napoleon was the subject of protracted negotiations during the six preceding months. It was no easy task to devise a ritual that would pay deference to older monarchical traditions, and yet incorporate an element of novelty to reflect the general's unorthodox rise to the throne. The Pope was eventually persuaded to attend and offer his blessing, but the religious dimension of the ceremony was undermined by Napoleon's unwillingness to take communion and, above all, his insistence that he crown himself as the supreme symbol of his self-made rather than God-given status.

It was a far cry from the coronations conducted at Reims for the kings of old. A secular celebration of Napoleon's authority followed the Pope's departure from the cathedral. Bonaparte took the following oath of allegiance:

I swear to maintain the integrity of the Republic's territory, to respect and cause to be respected the laws of the Concordat and the freedom of worship, equality of rights, civil and political liberty, the irrevocability of the sale of national property, neither to levy nor to introduce any tax, except in accordance with the law, to maintain the institution of the Legion of Honour (a title awarded for services rendered to the state that was introduced in 1802), and to govern with the sole aim of the interests, happiness and glory of the French people.

This incongruous list of promises, which continued to refer to the Republic, had already been violated by the new emperor, for little remained of freedom. The Revolution in France thus ended on a note of resignation rather than genuine celebration. Michelet, the great nineteenth-century French historian, was just six years old in 1804; later, he recalled having noticed nothing out of the ordinary on the momentous occasion of Napoleon's coronation, save for a 'mournful and dismal silence'.

The Emperor Napoleon I, as he now became, might still brag that the *coup d'état* effected on 18 Brumaire had saved the Republic, but after 1804 this was patently no longer the case. Indeed, the political liberties associated with the French Revolution were a casualty of his dictatorship from the moment he was made First Consul in 1800. The apprenticeship in democracy, which the First Republic had inspired, was brutally interrupted by the Bonapartist experiment, an episode that had far less lasting impact in the political than in the administrative sphere. To be sure, liberty led a charmed life during the revolutionary decade. Yet, so long as some form of representative government continued to exist under the Directory, there remained the possibility that freedom might be more fully embraced; after 18 Brumaire this prospect simply disappeared. In this sense, the triumph of Napoleon was a tragedy, both for France and for Europe.

Illustrative Documents

1. HISTORIOGRAPHY

The events which occurred in the past may not change, but historians' interpretations of them certainly do. This section demonstrates some of the different ways in which Napoleon's advent to power has been presented over the past two centuries.

DOCUMENT I Bonaparte's proclamation justifying the Brumaire *coup*, 10 November 1799

Bonaparte had a genius for propaganda and his version of the coup d'état *was published within hours of his appointment as Provisional Consul on 19 Brumaire (10 November 1799). Although this account was evidently an essay in self-justification, it has enjoyed enduring influence.*

On my return to Paris, I found division among all the authorities and agreement upon only one point, namely, that the Constitution was half-destroyed and unable to save liberty. All parties came to see me, and confided their plans to me, revealed their secrets, and requested my support; I refused to be the man of any party.

The Council of Elders summoned me; I responded to its call. A plan of general restoration had been put together by men whom the nation is accustomed to regard as defenders of liberty, equality and property: this plan required calm and independent scrutiny, free from all untoward influence and fear. The Council of Elders accordingly resolved to transfer the Legislative Body to Saint-Cloud; it gave me responsibility for organizing the force necessary for its independence. I believed it my duty to my fellow citizens, to the soldiers perishing in our armies, to the national glory bought with their blood, to accept the command.

The Councils assembled at Saint-Cloud; republican troops guaranteed their security from without, but assassins created terror inside. Several deputies from the Council of Five Hundred, armed with stilettos and firearms, surrounded them with threats of death. The plans which should have been developed were held up, the majority became disorganized, the most courageous speakers were disconcerted and the futility of every wise proposition was evident.

I took my indignation and grief to the Council of Elders. I demanded from it an assurance that its generous plans would be implemented; I directed its attention to the evils besetting the *patrie*, which had prompted them to act; it concurred with me by offering fresh evidence of its steadfast will.

I then presented myself at the Council of Five Hundred, alone, unarmed, head uncovered, in the same fashion as the Elders had received and applauded me. I came to remind the majority of its wishes and to assure it of its authority.

The stilettos which threatened the deputies were immediately raised against their liberator; twenty assassins threw themselves upon me and aimed at my chest. The grenadiers of the Legislative Body, whom I had left at the door of the hall, ran forward and interposed themselves between the assassins and myself. One of the grenadiers had his clothes pierced by a stiletto. They carried me out.

At the same moment, cries of 'Outlaw!' were raised against the defender of the law. It was the fierce cry of assassins against the force destined to put them down.

They pressed around the President of the Council, uttering threats, arms in their hands; they ordered him to declare me an outlaw; I was informed of this and ordered that he be snatched from their fury, and six grenadiers of the Legislative Body secured him. Immediately afterwards, some other grenadiers charged into the hall and cleared it.

Thus intimidated, the factions dispersed and fled. The majority, shielded from their attacks, returned freely and peaceably to the meeting hall, heard the propositions which were made for the public safety, discussed them, and prepared the salutary resolution which is to become the new and provisional law of the Republic.

Frenchmen, without doubt you will recognize in this conduct all the zeal of a soldier of liberty, a citizen devoted to the Republic. Conservative, tutelary and liberal ideas have been restored to their rightful place by the dispersal of the agitators who oppressed the

Councils and who, having become the most odious of men, have not ceased to be the most contemptible.

(Napoleon Bonaparte, *Correspondance de Napoléon 1er publiée par ordre de l'Empereur Napoléon III* (32 vols., Paris, 1858-69), vol.6, 6–8. Translated.)

DOCUMENT II   Count Albert Vandal on the advent of Napoleon

Napoleon continues to attract numerous apologists, albeit in the literary rather than the academic sphere, but few writers have ever matched the eloquence of the two volumes which Albert Vandal devoted to the advent of Bonaparte at the turn of the twentieth century. In this passage he takes issue with liberal critics of the coup d'état.

Among the accepted legends about 18 Brumaire, none is more erroneous than the supposition that it brought about the death of liberty. For a long time it was a historical commonplace to represent Bonaparte in the Council of Five Hundred at Saint-Cloud destroying a genuine legality with one stroke of his sword and drowning out with his drum rolls the last gasps of French liberty. Such solemn nonsense can no longer be repeated in face of some clearly recognized and understood facts. Bonaparte can be reproached for not having established liberty; he cannot be accused of having destroyed it, for the excellent reason that on his return from Egypt he did not find it anywhere in France. Bonaparte could not suppress something that did not exist. In the early days of the Directory, amid violent reactionary movements, tension had started to relax and a few liberties were recognized. The death of liberty came not on 18 Brumaire but on 18 Fructidor (4 September 1797), when the revolutionaries ruthlessly seized dictatorial power again to stop a resurgence of royalism. After this *coup d'état* against the nation, almost all the liberties constitutionally guaranteed to the French people were forcibly snatched away or treacherously withdrawn . . .

In 1789, people experienced a spontaneous anarchy; a decade later, in 1799, there was a spontaneous reaction against the Revolution that threatened to turn into another form of anarchy, a frenzy of reprisals and revenge . . .

It was against the other half of the republican party, against the Jacobins and demagogues, that the seizure of power was carried out; but Bonaparte had declared immediately after his victory that there were no vanquished, that he did not wish to know of any. To the purged legislators, to the Jacobins who 'showed the least sign of repentance', he very willingly awarded compensations and profitable, if obscure posts; he let those whom he had thrown out of the windows return by this humble back door. This manner of granting them amnesty was enough to soothe the irritation, to dress yesterday's wound; and the sword of Bonaparte assumed a resemblance to the lance of Achilles, which possessed the marvellous power to cure the wounds it inflicted . . .

The royalists, on the other hand, felt disappointed because they wanted more of a reaction. The harshness, especially the verbal harshness, directed against them, and the care taken by the Consuls to maintain in principle the laws of the Revolution and to declare that this set of laws was untouchable, rid them of any notion that there would be a very marked change; they said sadly: 'It is still the republic of the Revolution and not a national republic.' Even so, most continued to hope; they thought the new power, born of an anti-Jacobin movement, would end up sooner or later succumbing to the impulses which originated it, and that, despite everything, reaction was on the march . . .

Support for the new regime came especially from below; it came from the underlying strata of the population and went to Bonaparte personally without regard to colleagues and associates. His party, a party being formed, was all of France that was disgusted with politics and did not wish to have any more to do with it. It was a France of workers and ordinary folk, the innumerable mass of small property-owners, the people from the demi-bourgeoisie, those involved in industry and farming – the real people who should not be confused with either the Jacobin rabble or the demagogues of the Right. The strength of Bonaparte was to represent the opinion of those who previously had none, or no longer had one. These working people had not yet received any positive benefits from him. They liked him anyway, because they saw in him the embodiment of their hopes; they were grateful to him for what they expected from him. Although he lacked real means to act, his colossal reputation sustained him and inspired confidence in his future works.

(A. Vandal, *L'Avènement de Bonaparte* (2 vols., Paris, 1903-7), vol. 1, 26–7, 480–1, 484. Translated.)

DOCUMENT III Madame de Staël on Brumaire

Madame de Staël, an intellectual of Swiss origin, offers a good example of the liberal critique of Bonaparte's conduct in 1799. It is instructive to compare her account of the 18 Brumaire with that of Napoleon himself. Not surprisingly, de Staël left France shortly afterwards and this extract from her Considerations on the French Revolution was only published later, under the Bourbon Restoration.

The Revolution of 18 Brumaire

During the time that had elapsed since Bonaparte's brothers had written to him in Egypt, summoning him back, the state of affairs in France had changed a great deal . . . The English had invaded Holland, but they had already been thrown out. The Russians had been defeated at Zurich by Masséna, and the French armies had gone back on to the offensive in Italy. Thus, when General Bonaparte returned, Switzerland, Holland and Piedmont were all under French control once more; the barrier of the Rhine, conquered by the Republic, was no longer at issue and French forces had struck an equilibrium with the other states of Europe. Of all the possible outcomes available, France chose to take as leader the cleverest of the generals, who would conquer and subjugate the people. Tyranny even overwhelmed the armed forces for which so many sacrifices had been made.

It was not, therefore, the external reverses suffered by France that produced the fatal attraction to Bonaparte in 1799, but rather the fear inspired by the Jacobins inside the country which worked so powerfully in his favour. The Jacobins had few resources at their disposal and their reappearance was no more than a spectre which stirred in the ashes; but it was sufficient to revive the panic they had generated in the past and the nation threw itself into the arms of Bonaparte, simply to escape from a phantom . . .

When Caesar overthrew the Roman Republic he had to fight Pompey and the most illustrious patricians of the day. Cicero and Cato fought against him; there was a grandeur to the opposition. General Bonaparte, by contrast, encountered only adversaries whose names are not worth repeating . . .

Bonaparte met few obstacles on his way to power . . . Many different interpretations have been applied to the revolution of 18 Brumaire. It is especially important to note in these events the characteristic traits of the man who was to become master of the European continent for the next fifteen years. He went to the rostrum in the Council of Elders in an attempt to carry them along by addressing them in a friendly and decent fashion, but he did not know how to speak in the requisite language. It was not in polite conversation that his sharp mind worked to the best advantage; moreover, since he has no real concern for any particular issue, he is only eloquent in abuse and he finds nothing more difficult than to limit himself, without a script, to the sort of respectful approach needed for an assembly that has to be won over. He tried to say to the Council of Elders, 'I am the god of war and of fortune: follow me', but he used these words in an awkward fashion, because what he would really have liked to say was: 'You are a miserable bunch and I will have you shot if you do not do as I say' . . .

He then arrived in the Council of Five Hundred, arms crossed, with a very grim look on his face and accompanied by two tall grenadiers who were protecting his diminutive stature. The so-called Jacobin deputies let out howls of derision when they saw him enter the hall. His brother Lucien, who fortunately for him was president of the assembly, rang the bell in an attempt to restore order, but in vain. Cries of 'traitor' and 'usurper' could be heard in all quarters and one of the deputies, a Corsican compatriot of Bonaparte, Aréna, went up to the general, seized the lapels of his uniform and shook him. It was alleged, though without foundation, that he was wielding a dagger to kill him. At all events, this action startled Bonaparte and he said to the grenadiers who were at his side, as his head fell against the shoulder of one of them: 'Get me out of here' . . .

After General Bonaparte was taken out of the Council of Five Hundred . . . (he) hastened to send in the troops to rescue Lucien and take him to safety outside the assembly; as soon as he had left, the grenadiers entered the Orangery, where the deputies were gathered, and chased them out by marching forward from one end of the hall to the other, as if there was no-one there. The deputies, pinned against the walls, were obliged to escape by jumping out of the windows into the gardens of Saint-Cloud, still wearing their togas. The representatives of the French people had been proscribed on previous occasions, but this was the first time in the Revolution that the civilian authority had been humiliated by the military forces. Bonaparte, who wanted to base his power on the degradation of the Legislature . . . rejoiced in the fact that from the outset he had destroyed the credibility of the people's deputies . . .

(Madame de Staël, *Considérations sur la Révolution française*
(2 vols., Paris, 1818), vol.2, 4–9. Translated.)

DOCUMENT IV   Georges Lefebvre on the rise of Napoleon

Georges Lefebvre is one of the great twentieth-century historians of the Revolution and, like most of his academic counterparts, he is rather unsympathetic to Napoleon, whom he accuses of establishing a military dictatorship. However, writing from a Marxist perspective, rather than dwelling upon Bonaparte's vaulting ambition, Lefebvre emphasizes the impersonal forces that carried the general to power.

That the French Revolution turned to dictatorship was no accident; it was driven there by inner necessity, and not for the first time either. Nor was it an accident that the Revolution led to the dictatorship of a general, but it so happened that this general was Napoleon Bonaparte . . .

The people having been eliminated as an obstacle to the dictatorship of the bourgeoisie, only the army remained. The Directory had already sought its help on 18 Fructidor, Year V, and had managed to keep the upper hand, despite serious incursions. Now, however, the situation was very different in that steadfast republicans, not royalists, were to be driven out. Only a popular general could have carried it through, and Bonaparte's sudden return destined that it should be he. The will of the nation that was invoked to justify 18 Brumaire played no part in the event. The nation rejoiced at the news that Bonaparte was in France because it recognized an able general; but the Republic had conquered without him, and Masséna's victory had bolstered the reputation of the Directory. Consequently, the responsibility for 18 Brumaire lies with that segment of the republican bourgeoisie called the Brumairians, whose leading light was Sieyès. They had no intention of giving in to Bonaparte, and they chose him only as an instrument of their policy. That they propelled him to power without imposing any conditions, without even delimiting the fundamental character of the new regime, betrays their mediocrity. Bonaparte did not repudiate the *notables*, for he was not a democrat, and their collaboration alone enabled him to rule. But on the evening of 19 Brumaire, after they had hurriedly slapped together the structure of the Provisional Consulate, they should not have harboured any more illusions. The army had followed Bonaparte, and him alone. He was complete master. Regardless of what he and his apologists may have said, his rule was from its origins an absolute military dictatorship. It was Bonaparte alone who would decide the questions on which the fate of France and Europe hinged.

(Georges Lefebvre, Napoleon, trans. by Henry F. Stockhold (2 vols.,
London, 1969), vol.1, 60, 62–3.)

DOCUMENT V   Martyn Lyons on Brumaire

Anglo-Saxon historians have generally taken a more detached view of Napoleon, mixing admiration and criticism, while not neglecting the general circumstances in which Bonaparte seized power. Martyn Lyons is a current specialist who strikes a judicious balance between these elements in his recent account of the coup d'état.

The Directory had lasted four years and was the longest survivor of all the regimes of the First French Republic. Thanks to Bonaparte and its generals it had pursued the war against the First Coalition with some success. It had defeated royalist threats and was beginning to pull the Republic out of financial chaos. Yet the Republic had paid a high price for the Directory's survival. The government's manipulation of electoral results had discredited republican politics and destroyed credibility in the Constitution of the Year 3. By 1799, the Directory looked increasingly like a temporary solution that was already out of date. The military defeats and internal insurrections of that year made constitutional revision even more imperative . . .

Brumaire, then, did not announce the end of the principles of the French Revolution. It signified rather that one particular institutional form of those revolutionary ideals had served out its usefulness, and succumbed to history. The revolutionary bourgeois of France had spent four years navigating a dangerous passage between the perils of a royalist restoration and Jacobin-led economic controls. They needed to defend their gains, the abolition of the monarchy and of aristocratic privilege, and they needed an assurance that the end of seigneurialism and the sale of *biens nationaux* were definitive. The Directory no longer provided a sufficient guarantee; they turned to the new set of institutions to protect the legacy of the French Revolution. The *coup* of Brumaire may best be interpreted not as a rupture with the immediate revolutionary past, but as a new attempt to secure and prolong the hegemony of the revolutionary bourgeoisie. It was ironic that the French bourgeoisie, usually so timid, concerned with stability and wary of risk, had entrusted the Revolution to a diminutive Corsican soldier and his creole wife from Martinique, who had offered herself to the Directorial élite as one of the spoils of power.

(Martyn Lyons, *Napoleon Bonaparte and the Legacy of the French Revolution* (Basingstoke, 1994), 29 and 41–2.)

2. THE ROAD TO BRUMAIRE

The 'black legend' of the Directory that was largely created by the Bonapartist regime after 1799 has all too often been accepted at face value. The extracts that follow reveal the great difficulties that the Directory confronted, as well as its efforts to overcome them.

DOCUMENT VI   Proclamation issued by the Directors after their installation in November 1795

The five-man executive Directory inherited a difficult situation when it was established in November 1795, following adoption of the Constitution of the Year III. The problems stemming from six years of revolutionary upheaval, which are mentioned here, were to plague the new government during the years that immediately followed. Many of the lofty objectives set out in this inaugural manifesto – remarkably similar to those proclaimed by Bonaparte four years later – were not to be achieved, but it would be wrong to assume that this latest attempt to end the Revolution was inevitably doomed to failure from the outset.

Frenchmen, the executive Directory has just been installed. Determined to maintain liberty or die, it is firmly resolved to consolidate the Republic and to give all necessary dispatch and vigour to the Constitution.

Republicans, rest assured, its destiny will never be separated from yours; inflexible justice and the strictest observance of the laws will be its rule. To wage an active war on royalism, to rekindle patriotism, to repress all factions vigorously, to extinguish all party spirit, to remove every desire for vengeance, to establish concord, to restore peace, to regenerate morals, to resuscitate the sources of production, to revive commerce and industry, to stifle speculation, to revivify the arts and sciences, to re-establish plenty and the public credit, to reinstate public order in place of the chaos that inevitably accompanies revolutions and, finally, to obtain for the French Republic all the happiness and glory which it awaits – such is the task of your legislators and of the executive Directory: it will be its constant preoccupation and everyone's major concern. Wise laws, promptly and energetically enforced, will soon put paid to our prolonged sufferings.

But the suppression of so many evils and the creation of so much good cannot be achieved overnight. The French people are fair-minded and loyal; they will realize that, in view of the confused circumstances in which we have assumed political responsibility, we need time, calm, patience and confidence equal to the efforts we shall have to make. Such confidence will not be betrayed if the people cease to allow themselves to be won over by the perfidious promises of royalists who are resuming their plots, of fanatics who are constantly inflaming opinions, and of public bloodsuckers who always take advantage of our misfortunes. It will not be betrayed if the people do not attribute to the new authorities the disorders caused by six years of revolution, which will inevitably take time to redress . . .

Frenchmen, do not hinder the work of a newborn government . . . on the contrary, give your support to the ever-active efforts and the imperturbable progress of the executive Directory towards the prompt establishment of public happiness; and soon, bearing the glorious title of republicans, you will irrevocably ensure national peace and prosperity.

(Le directoire exécutif au peuple français, 14 Brumaire IV (5 November 1795), *Moniteur* 19 Brumaire IV (10 November 1795). Translated.)

DOCUMENT VII   Louis XVIII's declaration from Verona, 1795

Louis XVIII became pretender to the French throne in 1795, but immediately disappointed more moderate royalists with this Declaration from Italy, where he was in exile. As this extract shows, his vision of a monarchical restoration was founded on the old order. There was little scope for compromise with revolutionary principles where religion, politics and society were concerned.

Louis, by the grace of God, King of France and Navarre

To all our subjects, Greeting . . .

Impiety and revolt have been the cause of all the torments you experience: in order to stop their progress you must dry up their source. You must renounce the dominion of those treacherous and cruel usurpers who promised you happiness, but who have given you only famine and death: we wish to relieve you from their tyranny, which has so much injured you, to inspire you with the resolution of shaking it off. You must return to that holy religion which showered down on France the blessings of Heaven. We wish to restore its altars; by prescribing justice to sovereigns and fidelity to subjects, it maintains good order, ensures the triumph of the laws and produces the fidelity of empires. You must restore that government which, for fourteen centuries, constituted the glory of France and the delight of her inhabitants; which rendered our country the most flourishing of states and yourselves the happiest of people: it is our wish to restore it. Have not the various revolutions which have occurred only increased your distress, since the period of its destruction, and convinced you that it is the only government that is fit for you?

Give no credit to those rapacious and ambitious men who, in order to violate your property and to engross all power, have told you that France had no constitution, or, at least, that its constitution was despotic. Its existence is as ancient as the monarchy of the Franks; it is the product of genius, the masterpiece of wisdom, and the fruit of experience. In composing the body of the French people of three distinct orders, it traced with precision that scale of subordination without which society cannot exist . . .

(Translation printed in the British *Annual Register* (July, 1795), 253–6.)

DOCUMENT VIII   The Babeuf plot, 1796

There was uncompromising opposition to the Directory from Left as well as Right. The most famous radical challenge to the regime emanated from the Babeuf plot, though its significance grew far greater in the future. In 1796, the plot was uncovered and promptly suppressed. Its leader, the revolutionary journalist, 'Gracchus' Babeuf, was executed, but this first 'communist manifesto' acquired lasting influence as a precursor of later movements.

The Manifesto of the Equals

The French Revolution is only the forerunner of another, even greater revolution that will finally put an end to the era of revolutions. The people have swept away the Kings and priests who have been in league against them. Next they will sweep away the modern upstarts, the tyrants and tricksters who have usurped the ancient seats of power.

What else do we need other than equality before the law? We need not only this equality as it is written down in the Declaration of the Rights of Man and the Citizen; we need it in our life, in our very midst, in our homes. For the true and living equality we will give up everything. Let the arts perish, if need be! But let us have real equality.

Men of high degree – lawmakers, rulers, the rich – strangers as you are to the love of man, to good faith, to compassion: it is no good to say that we are only 'bringing up again the old cry of *loi agraire*' [literally 'agrarian law', an equal division of the land]. It is our turn to speak. Listen to our just demands and to the law of nature which sanctions them. The *loi agraire* has been the instinctive demand of a handful of soldiers of fortune, of peoples here and there governed by passion, not by reason. We intend something far better and far more just; the COMMON GOOD or the COMMUNITY OF GOODS. There must be an end to individual ownership of the land, for *the land is nobody's personal property*. Our demand is for the communal ownership of the earth's resources. *These resources are the property of mankind.*

We say that an end must be put to the situation in which the overwhelming majority of mankind, living under the thumb of a tiny majority, sweats and toils for the sole benefit of a few.

In France fewer than a million persons own and dispose of wealth that rightfully belongs to twenty million of their fellow men, to their fellow citizens. There must be an end to this outrage!

. . . PEOPLE OF FRANCE, Open your eyes and and hearts to full happiness; recognize the REPUBLIC OF EQUALITY. Join us in working for it.

(Sylvain Maréchal, *Manifeste des Égaux*, 1796, reprinted from John Anthony Scott (ed.), *The Defense of Gracchus Babeuf* (New York, 1972), 91–5.)

DOCUMENT IX   Addresses from the Jacobins in 1799

More moderate left-wing opponents of the Directory gathered in constitutional circles and, as their name suggests, sought to work within the existing political framework. Their windy rhetoric, which called for draconian measures against enemies of the Republic, none the less inspired great fear among solid property owners and provided a justification for the emergency measures taken by Napoleon and his fellow conspirators in 1799.

(a) Citizens comprising the Society of the Friends of Liberty and Equality at Périgueux

Legislators . . . Never cease to resist those wicked men who wish to inspire fear and sow dissension among you; provide constant protection for Republicans, prompt retribution for the crimes of the triumvirate [the three directors who had recently been removed from office] and the depredations of its numerous lackeys; speed up the manufacture of weapons by all possible means; pay no attention to the howls of avarice and corruption – ensure that the forced loan is levied without delay; do you regard as friends of the Republic those who allow their own interests to outweigh those of the *patrie?* No, such persons deserve to be nothing but slaves, their contemptible behaviour only benefits royalism, as we are all well aware. Amidst the crises of the Revolution, the persistent slanderers of the patriotic societies never cease to search for means to blunt, even shatter that sacred enthusiasm that makes them tremble so much. The accomplices of Pitt may try to trample upon the Constitution, but all Frenchmen worthy of the name will rise up to resist them.

(b) The citizens of Dun-sur-Auron, department of the Cher

Public opinion has been pulled in all directions by royalism and fanaticism. All sorts of crimes against liberty have been permitted. Defenders of the *patrie* have been diverted fron the path of duty, the Friends of the Republic have been dispersed, slandered and assassinated. The most absurd rumours have been put into circulation in order to snuff out public resolve, lower the citizens' morale and turn them from the new institutions. Such are the ills that you have to combat, the evils to which you must put an end. May liberty crush its enemies like a thunderbolt!

(c) Members of the Reunion Club at Mende, in the department of the Lozère

We are awaiting justice and vengeance from you. In vain the enemies of liberty are spreading abroad wicked ideas of reaction and terror, in order to prevent the implementation of laws which circumstances have demanded, and to deprive the executive Directory of all the suitable means for repulsing the coalition of kings and preventing internal breakdown which can only issue in civil war. They will not succeed, for we know that our constitution enshrines the guarantee of our rights, that it is the touchstone guiding our legislative body and that you will only strike at guilty parties so as to defend this same constitution . . . Hand over to the blade of justice those public leeches whose very existence is a disgrace to all republicans; seek out those scandalous fortunes which have been swollen by the sweat of our fellow citizens; punish those petty tyrants who, in the sister republics founded by our warriors, would have dishonoured the French name were it possible to tarnish such a glorious title.

(Addresses sent to the Legislative Councils in July 1799, cited in Jean-Paul Bertaud, *Bonaparte prend le pouvoir* (Brussels, 1987), 128–30. Translated.)

DOCUMENT X   The Executive Directory issues advice for the elections of the Year VI (March–April 1798)

The Directory itself had not shied away from unconstitutional action to frustrate right- and then left-wing successes at the elections of 1797 and 1798. In this extraordinary proclamation, issued just before the departmental electoral assemblies met in April 1798, the Minister of the Interior promised to annul any untoward results. His threat was duly fulfilled when numerous newly elected deputies were rejected in the so-called coup d'état of Floréal VI (May 1798).

Citizens,

A vast conspiracy, skilfully plotted, ensured that the choice of the electors in the Year V (1797) fell upon out-and-out royalists. The efforts of your legislators, faithful to their task, struck down the conspirators and overthrew their odious project.

This year, ever true to their objective of overturning the Republic, our foreign foes have changed their tack, but not their intentions. They have conjured up a different sort of conspiracy with no less audacity and just as much treachery. Their aim is to put universally detested individuals into the legislature and local office, men whose very names terrify both the silent majority and firm republicans alike. The names of persons with an infamous record in the annals of the revolution are already to be found on the lists of second-degree electors. The project, which they do not hide, is to strike terror into the hearts of all citizens and to encourage them to take their fortunes out of the country.

Citizens, rest assured, the government is on the alert; it knows the enemies who are troubling the country; their plots will be foiled. On 18 Fructidor (September 1797) the legislative body knew just how to rid its ranks of traitors who had been sitting there for four months; it is quite prepared to exclude those who might be elected now. It disposes of the authority to validate the operations of the electoral assemblies. That power will be duly exercised in Floréal [May] and you can be sure that its sense of justice, its commitment to the constitution and its devotion to the Republic will set a seal of disapproval upon any choices that the conspirators have dictated by means of violence, intrigue, cabals and illegal influence.

For too long the factions have troubled France. Calm and confidence must be restored. It is essential that agriculture, trade and the arts flourish again and that all the sources of public prosperity are restored amongst us. Such is the wish of all the true friends of liberty and it is also the constant preoccupation of the government. Citizens, you can count on its zeal and courage. Strengthened by the support of pure and faithful republicans in the legislature and by the will of the people who entrusted the defence of the constitution to it, it takes, before the heavens and before the whole nation, a solemn oath to remove from the territory of the Republic all brigands, to whichever party they belong, behind whatever mask they are hiding and wherever they are to be found.

(Merlin de Douai, for the executive Directory, *Moniteur* 11 Germinal VI
(31 March 1798). Translated.)

3. BRUMAIRE

The extracts in this section not only reveal how the coup *was executed, with contributions from two of the key players; they also show how news of these dramatic events was transmitted to the French public and suggest some of the reactions.*

DOCUMENT XI   Barras offers his excuses

Barras had served as a Director since the inception of the regime in 1795. His resignation on 18 Brumaire (9 November 1799) was crucial to the collapse of executive authority and to the subsequent success of the coup. Naturally he sought to exculpate himself in his unreliable memoirs, which were not published until the end of the nineteenth century. Though he fails to mention the personal compensation that rewarded his premature retirement, he was probably correct to suggest that resistance would have been futile.

Brumaire, Year VIII

I have narrated truthfully, I may even say with candour, all that I did in the course of events leading up to the 18th Brumaire; nor have I concealed that on the day itself I may perhaps have incurred grave censure, whether I be charged with having forgotten all my revolutionary experience and with having been wanting in foresight, or whether it is argued that I lacked firmness on the day itself by appearing not to resist the actual event. Nevertheless, those who possess an accurate knowledge of the state of things and of persons at that juncture are capable of themselves estimating the bearing of any efforts I might have made. I was perhaps really tired of a lengthy tenure of office, and even of the result of victories I had found myself in the necessity of winning over the various factions opposed to us . . .

Hence, to speak in a precise fashion and without seeking to conceal anything of my individuality in this affair, I ask my most persistent accusers what they imagine I should have accomplished had I ridden into the Faubourg Saint-Antoine or to the *corps législatif*. Who would have followed me when all the civil, military, and even suburban populations, for so long worked upon, were rushing towards Bonaparte as if towards a fresh existence? Will those who had for so long brought me into disrepute and rendered me so unpopular, blame me for not having employed the forces they had deprived me of? These forces, I confess, I no longer possessed; if they supported and accompanied me in all preceding revolutions, I have always recognized that I had been victorious only because I had the people on my side and went onward with them.

At the time of the 18th Brumaire where can the people be said to have been, when the Council of Five Hundred itself did not know whither to turn? . . .

(*Memoirs of Barras*, edited by George Duruy and translated by Charles E. Roche (4 vols., London, 1896), vol.IV, 132–4.)

DOCUMENT XII   Bonaparte's speech to the Council of Elders, 19 Brumaire VIII (10 November 1799)

Angered by the failure of the Legislative Councils to enact emergency measures more quickly, once they had reassembled at Saint-Cloud on 19 Brumaire (10 November), Bonaparte rashly attempted to speed things up. The home truths he related were not well received by the Elders and his appearance in the Council of Five Hundred almost brought the coup *to grief, though such resistance helped to legitimate the events that followed.*

Citizen Representatives, the situation in which you find yourselves is far from normal; you are sitting on top of a volcano.

Permit me to speak to you with the frankness of a soldier and, in order to escape the trap which is set for you, suspend your judgement until I have finished what I have to say.

Yesterday, I was peacefully in Paris when you summoned me to notify me of the decree of transfer and charge me with its execution. I immediately assembled my comrades and we flew to your aid. Well! Today slanders are heaped upon me. There is talk of Caesar, of Cromwell, of military government. If I had wanted military government, would I have rushed to lend my support to the representative body of the nation?

Citizen Representatives, time is short; it is essential that you act quickly. The Republic no longer has a government. Four of the Directors have resigned; I have deemed it necessary to place the fifth under surveillance, by virtue of the power you have conferred upon me. The Council of Five Hundred is divided; only the Council of Elders remains. From it I hold my powers. Let it take action, let it speak: I am here to carry out its will. Together let us save the cause of liberty and equality!

[A cry: 'And the Constitution?']

The Constitution! You have destroyed it yourselves. You violated it on 18 Fructidor; you violated it on 22 Floréal; you violated it on 30 Prairial. No one respects it any longer. I will speak openly. Since my return, I have not ceased to be surrounded by intrigue. Every faction hastened to embrace me. Men who insolently call themselves 'the only patriots' came to tell me that the constitution must be set aside; to purify the councils, they proposed to exclude men who are sincere friends of the *patrie*. This is their attachment to the Constitution! I became fearful for the Republic. I joined with my brothers in arms;

and we have come to form our ranks around you. There is no time to lose; let the Council of Elders pronounce. I am not an intriguer; you know me; I believe I have given enough proofs of my devotion to the *patrie*. Those who speak to you of the Constitution well know that, violated at every moment, mutilated at every page, the Constitution no longer exists. The sovereignty of the people, liberty and equality, these sacred foundations of the Constitution, still remain: they must be saved. If by Constitution one means these sacred principles, all the rights belonging to the people, all those belonging to each citizen, my comrades and I are ready to shed our blood to defend them. But I will not prostitute the meaning of a constitutional act by applying the term to purely administrative regulations which offer the citizen no guarantee. As for what follows, I declare that once this is over I shall be nothing in the Republic but the arm supporting what you have established.

Citizen Representatives, the Council of Five Hundred is divided; the factional leaders have brought this about. The men of Prairial, who wish to bring back to the soil of liberty the scaffolds and the horrible regime of the Terror, are surrounding themselves with their accomplices and preparing to carry out their frightful plans. Already the Council of Elders is being blamed for the measures it has taken and for placing its trust in me. For my part, I am not shaken. Should I tremble before conspirators, I whom the coalition could not destroy? If I am a traitor, may you all be Brutus. And as for you, my comrades who accompany me, you, brave grenadiers whom I see surrounding this place, may these bayonets with which we have triumphed together be turned immediately against my heart. But also, should any orator in foreign pay dare pronounce against your general the word 'Outlaw' let the thunder of war crush him instantly. Remember that I march accompanied by the god of war and the god of fortune.

I withdraw . . . You will proceed to deliberate. Command, and I will carry out your orders.

[Many voices: 'Give us names! Give us names!']

Each had his ideas; each had his plans; each had his group and associates. Citizen Barras and Citizen Moulin [both Directors] had theirs. They made propositions to me.

[Many voices: 'The General Committee']

There is no longer any need for the General Committee; the whole of

France must learn what we wish to make known; we would be the most unworthy of men if we did not immediately take all the measures that can save liberty and equality.

Since my arrival, all the magistrates and officials with whom I have spoken have demonstrated to me their conviction that the Constitution, so frequently violated and continually disregarded, is headed towards destruction; that it offers the French people no guarantee because it lacks a firm basis. All the factions are convinced of this; all are ready to profit from the fall of the present government; all have come to me; all have wished to win me over to their side. I have felt it my duty to unite only with the Council of Elders, the first body of the Republic. I repeat to you that you cannot act too promptly, if you wish to stop the movement which is going to kill liberty, perhaps in an instant.

Deliberate, Citizen Representatives, I have just told you some home truths that everyone has whispered to himself, but that someone must finally have the courage to say out loud. The means of saving the *patrie* are in your hands; if you hesitate to use them, if liberty perishes, you will answer for it before the universe, before posterity, before France and your families.

[The general withdraws.]

(Napoleon, *Correspondance*, vol. 6, 3–6. Translated.)

DOCUMENT XIII   Decree replacing the Executive Directory with the Provisional Consulate, 19 Brumaire VIII (10 November 1799)

In order to lend the military coup a semblance of legality, scattered remnants of the Five Hundred were reassembled to vote the emergency decree contained in this extract. Dictated by the conspirators, these measures were subsequently endorsed by surviving deputies in the Council of Elders, as the legislative procedure required.

The Council of Five Hundred . . . considering the situation of the Republic . . . approves the act of urgency and the following resolution:

1. The Directory no longer exists and the individuals named herein are no longer members of the national representation, because of the excesses and crimes to which they have constantly been prone

and, above all, the conduct of most of them at this morning's session. [Sixty-one names are attached.]

2. The Legislative Body provisionally creates an Executive Consular Commission, composed of citizens Sieyès and Roger Ducos, ex-Directors and Bonaparte, general, who will bear the title 'Consuls of the Republic'.

3. This Commission is invested with the plenitude of directorial power and is specially charged with organizing order throughout the administration, of re-establishing domestic peace and with obtaining an honourable and stable peace abroad.

4. It is authorized to send deputies, with fixed powers, throughout the country.

5. The Legislative Body will adjourn until 1 Ventôse [20 February 1800]; at that time it will reconvene in its usual meeting places.

6. During the adjournment of the Legislative Body, the adjourned deputies will retain their salaries and their constitutional immunity.

7. Without losing their status as representatives of the people they may be appointed ministers, diplomatic agents, deputies of the Executive Consular Commission and all other civil functions. For the public good they are even encouraged to accept them.

8. Before adjournment, and with immediate effect, each chamber will name from within its own ranks a commission composed of twenty-five members.

9. The commissioners named by the two chambers will make laws, with the formal and necessary approval of the Executive Consular Commission on all urgent matters of police, legislation and finance.

10. The Commission from the Five Hundred will exercise the initiative, that of the Elders consent.

11. The two commissions are also charged to prepare, according to the same arrangements of initiative and approval, a series of changes to be made to the Constitution of 1795, the weaknesses and inconveniences of which are well known through experience.

12. These changes can only have the objective of consolidating, guaranteeing and inviolably consecrating the sovereignty of the French people, the Republic one and indivisible, the representative system, the division of powers, and liberty, equality, security and property.

13. The Executive Consular Commission may present its views on these matters.

14. Finally, the two commissions are charged with preparing a civil code.

15. They will sit in Paris in the chambers of the legislative body, which they may convoke in special session for the ratification of peace, or in the event of serious public danger.

16. The present decree will be printed, sent by special couriers to the departments, and solemnly published and posted in all communes of the Republic.

Signed, Lucien Bonaparte, president, Emile Gaudin and Bara, secretaries.

After a second reading the Council of Elders approved the above resolution at Saint-Cloud, 19 Brumaire, Year VIII of the Republic [10 November 1799]. Signed, Joseph Cornudet, ex-president, Herwyn and P.-C. Laussat, secretaries.

> (Thierry Lentz, *Le 18-Brumaire: les coups d'état de Napoléon Bonaparte (novembre–décembre 1799)* (Paris, 1997), 457–60. Translated.)

DOCUMENT XIV   Advice to an opponent of the coup

The conspirators had a good deal of persuading to do after they had seized power on 19 Brumaire (10 November 1799). In this extract, Napoleon is personally attempting to win over Beyts, deputy for one of the recently annexed Belgian departments and an opponent of the coup. In this case the appeal to solidarity over factionalism proved a success and Beyts was integrated into the new regime.

Citizen, I have just received the letter you sent me on 27 Brumaire [18 November 1799]. Why have you taken such offence at events which have uniquely benefited the cause of order, liberty and enlightenment? The incident itself is over and I have no doubt that you will hasten to resume the role that a distinguished scholar like yourself should occupy, distant as you are from all spirit of party that the public good so much abhors.

I remember reading an extremely good report you wrote for the ratification of the treaty of Campo Formio, which permanently settled the future of your country, Belgium. No sensible person can think that the peace for which Europe still yearns will emerge from the factions and the disorganization they create. Everyone ought to join the great mass of the people. The simple title of French citizen is certainly worth more than that of royalist, Clichyen, Jacobin, Feuillant, and those thousand and one denominations that the spirit of faction produces and which, for the past ten years, have tended to hurl the nation into an abyss from which the time has finally come to rescue it for ever. All my efforts will be directed towards this goal. Henceforth that alone will earn the esteem of all right-thinking men, the respect of the people, and glory.

> (Napoleon, *Correspondance*, vol.6, 14–15. Letter written by Napoleon, on 3 Frimaire VIII (24 November 1799), to Beyts. Translated.)

DOCUMENT XV   A proclamation from the Provisional Consulate

An emphasis on the evils of party allegiance and the need for national unity forms a dominant motif in all the official proclamations issued by the Provisional Consulate. Equally characteristic is the promise to fulfil the original goals of the Revolution.

The Constitution of the Year III was dying. It could neither guarantee your rights, nor assure its own existence. Repeated assaults were robbing it irreparably of the people's respect. Malevolent, greedy factions were dividing up the Republic. France was finally approaching the last stage of a general disorganization.

Patriots have come together. All that could harm you has been set aside. All that could serve you, all that remained pure in the national representation has united under the banner of liberty.

Frenchmen, the Republic, strengthened and restored to that rank in Europe which it should never have lost, will see the realization of its citizens' hopes and the fulfilment of its glorious destiny.

Swear with us the oath we are taking to be faithful to the Republic, one and indivisible, founded upon liberty, equality and the representative system.

The Consuls of the Republic: Bonaparte, Roger Ducos and Sieyès, 21 Brumaire VIII [12 November 1799].

> (Napoleon, *Correspondance*, vol.6, 8–9. Translated.)

DOCUMENT XVI   A Napoleonic envoy at Marseilles
defends the *coup*

Envoys were dispatched to convey news of the coup *into the provinces, to
reinforce the message contained in official proclamations. The appeal to
national interest and revolutionary ideals was varied to suit the particular
audience, in this case the deeply divided Mediterranean city of Marseilles,
where war as well as revolution had ruined commercial prosperity.*

Citizens, the Republic was torn apart by the factions, an outrageous
struggle divided both legislature and executive, the armies were
deprived of essential equipment, the public revenues had dried up;
property was at risk; commerce was destroyed.

In this state of crisis, men renowned for the services they had
rendered to the Revolution and for their constant devotion to the
cause of freedom, formulated a plan for picking up the pieces of a
government on the point of collapse and for putting the
constitutional edifice on to firm foundations. They intend to do this
within a new political framework that will in future guarantee the
citizen's individual freedom, his property and the fruits of his
industry . . .

The sovereignty of the people, liberty, equality and the
representative system: these are the foundations upon which the
constitutional charter will be based. Can any republican entertain
the least misgiving in these circumstances? After all, the revolution of
19 Brumaire has already earned the approval of the army and near-
unanimity among the citizenry. There are no doubt, albeit in small
number, those who are seeking to spread alarm concerning this
memorable *journée*, together with regrets for the Constitution of the
Year III. They dare to suggest that the monarchy will be restored.
What blasphemy! No, the hideous throne has been abolished for ever
in France and the presence of a despot will never defile the land of
liberty.

Such people are regretting the passing of the Constitution of the
Year III. Yet in good faith it must be agreed that this Constitution,
which they themselves so vigorously denounced before 19 Brumaire
and which they wanted to replace with that of 1793, was deeply
flawed. Each year it produced political upheaval which set all the
parties at each other's throats, awakened all sorts of passionate
hatreds and threw the French people into a state of convulsion that
destroyed the happiness and repose of every citizen . . .

No, there will be no reaction. Henceforth, party labels and odious affiliations will be banned. Everyone will be invited to sacrifice their particular hatreds and resentments on the altar of the *patrie*. All desires and opinions will be united for the health and prosperity of the Republic.

(Fabre de l'Aude, consular emissary to the eighth military division, speaking at Marseilles on 23 Frimaire VIII (14 December 1799). Cited in Edmond Poupé, *Le Département du Var 1790 – an VIII* (Cannes, 1933), 492–5. Translated.)

DOCUMENT XVII   Some provincial reactions to Brumaire

After Brumaire, as at earlier points in the Revolution, a flood of declarations was dispatched to the new government by the local authorities. Though it is inadvisable to take these addresses at face value, they do indicate the extent to which Bonapartist propaganda had been absorbed in the provinces and the hopes for stability and security that the new government was expected to fulfil.

(a) The ruin of trade, the annihilation of the public finances, the exhaustion of all the resources of government, the protection accorded to corruption and systematic theft from the state, the denuding of our arsenals, stockpiles and citadels, the destitution experienced by our soldiers, widespread assassinations and brigandage in the countryside, the revival of civil war, the lack of enforcement of the law, the complete shambles in the administration, the Constitution violated by the different parties who have come to power and the ever-present threat of fresh upheaval. In short, the whole situation left us desperately hoping that the Republic might be plucked from the abyss into which ineptitude and betrayal had plunged us; we have every confidence that it will be.

The Central Administration of the department of the Isère, 25 Brumaire VIII [16 November 1799].

(b) The competence of the government had been wearing thin for a long time; the various branches of the administration offered only chaos; the political system no longer operated according to any clear design. From this state of uncertainty emanated only chaos and incoherence in the laws, which were merely a short-term response to the needs of the moment and either bore the imprint of impermanence or threatened further upheaval. The situation was guaranteed to embitter rather than win over the hearts and minds of the people.

For ten years France was the plaything of different factions . . . This state of affairs could endure no longer; 18 Brumaire will bring it to a close; the reign of the factions is over.

The Central Administration of the Ardèche, 1 Frimaire VIII [22 November 1799].

(c) We remained silent in face of the succession of *journées* that dealt a series of blows to the Constitution of the Year III, but our response to the events of 18 and 19 Brumaire is rather different. The character of the men who have carried it out promises us a brighter future . . . It is now up to you, legislators, to repair the flaws in the former constitution, by giving us a new one that will finally establish liberty on firm foundations . . .

The Municipal Administration of Saint-Vallier, in the department of the Drôme, 14 Frimaire VIII [5 December 1799].

(Archives nationales C595, Adresses au Corps législatif, Brumaire–Frimaire VIII (November–December 1799). Translated.)

4. THE CONSULATE

As the Revolution had shown, seizing power in Paris was one thing, but successfully establishing a new regime in France was quite another. Napoleon succeeded in consolidating his authority through the judicious mixture of reconciliatory and repressive measures represented here.

DOCUMENT XVIII   Extracts from the Constitution of the Year VIII

The rapid publication of a fresh constitution, that of the Year VIII from which these extracts are taken, bore testimony to the ideal of constitutional government established by the Revolution. Yet what stands out here, the restoration of a virtually universal male suffrage notwithstanding, is the domination of the consular executive over the Legislative Body and, above all, the ascendancy of the First Consul, Napoleon Bonaparte.

Title 1. Exercise of the rights of citizenship

1. The French Republic is one and indivisible. Its European territory is divided into departments and *arrondissements.*

2. Every man fully twenty-one years of age, born and resident in France, who has been enrolled upon the civic register of his *arrondissement* and has lived for the past year on the territory of the Republic, is a French citizen . . .

Title 2. The Conservative Senate

15. The Conservative Senate will be composed of eighty members. Senators will be at least forty years old; they are irremovable and hold office for life.

16. Appointment to the position of senator will be made by the Senate, which will choose from among three candidates presented by the Legislative Body, the Tribunate and the First Consul respectively . . .

20. The Senate will choose all legislators, tribunes, consuls, appeal judges and auditors.

21. The Senate will endorse or reject all acts referred to it as unconstitutional by the Tribunate or the government . . .

Title 3. Legislative power

25. New laws will be promulgated only when the draft bill has been proposed by the government, communicated to the Tribunate and decreed by the Legislative Body . . .

27. The Tribunate will be composed of 100 members, all of them at least twenty-five years old; they will be renewed annually by one-fifth and will be indefinitely re-eligible, as long as they remain on the national list.

28. The Tribunate will discuss draft bills; it will then decide to adopt or reject them . . .

31. The Legislative Body will comprise 300 members, of at least thirty years of age; they will be renewed annually by one-fifth. The Legislative Body must always include at least one citizen from each and every department of the Republic . . .

34. The Legislative Body will make laws by secret ballot, without any discussion on the part of its members, and on the basis of draft bills argued before it by speakers from the Tribunate and government . . .

Title 4. The government

39. The government will be entrusted to three Consuls, appointed for ten years and indefinitely re-eligible. Each will be elected separately, under the denomination of First, Second or Third Consul. The Constitution appoints as First Consul Citizen *Bonaparte*, former Provisional Consul; as Second Consul Citizen *Cambacérès* former minister of justice; and as Third Consul Citizen *Lebrun*, former member of the commission of the Council of Elders. On this occasion the Third Consul is appointed for a term of five years only.

40. The First Consul will have special functions and prerogatives in which he may be replaced temporarily by one of his colleagues when necessary.

41. The First Consul will promulgate laws; he will appoint and dismiss at will members of the Council of State, ministers, ambassadors and other external agents in chief, officers in the army and navy, members of the local administrations and the commissioners of the government in the courts. He will appoint all criminal and civil judges, other than justices of the peace and judges at the appeal court, without power to remove them.

42. In other acts of the government, the Second and Third Consuls will have a consultative voice; they will sign the register of such acts in order to attest their presence and, if they wish, they may record their opinions therein, after which the decision of the First Consul alone will stand.

43. The stipend of the First Consul will be 500,000 francs in the Year VIII. That of each of the other two Consuls will be three-fifths that of the First Consul . . .

(Godechot, *Les Constitutions de la France*, 151–7. Translated.)

DOCUMENT XIX   Presentation of the Constitution of the Year VIII to the French people, 5 Nivôse VIII (15 December 1799)

In putting the Constitution of the Year VIII to a referendum early in 1800, Napoleon was following revolutionary precedent. The claim that a constitutional settlement of this sort would mark the end of the Revolution had been made several times before; on this occasion it would be honoured, though the 'true principles of representative government' were casualties in the process.

Frenchmen!

A Constitution is presented to you. It ends the uncertainties that the Provisional Government brought into external relations, and into the internal and military situation of the Republic. It places in the institutions which it is establishing, leading magistrates whose commitment is necessary for its success. The Constitution is founded upon the true principles of representative government, upon the sacred rights of property, equality and liberty. The powers which it institutes will be strong and stable, as they must be to guarantee the rights of citizens and the interests of the state.

Citizens! The Revolution is established upon the principles with which it began: it is over.

(Napoleon, *Correspondance*, vol.6, 14–15. Translated.)

DOCUMENT XX   Some views on the Constitution of the Year VIII

Voters were simply invited to indicate acceptance or rejection of the constitution, but the habit of offering a more detailed opinion was deeply ingrained among the French electorate. As these extracts from the Mediterranean department of the Var demonstrate, many statements were made which afford further insight into public opinion in the wake of Napoleon's coup d'état, both for and against.

(a) I, the undersigned, considering that the Constitution of the French Republic, issued on 22 Frimaire Year VIII [13 December 1799], is based on a representative government, which signals the death of anarchy and will associate liberty with good order, peace and respect for persons and property, declare that I accept the said Constitution.

(b) I, the undersigned, accept the Constitution of the Year VIII. I rejoiced at the return of citizen Bonaparte, I was overjoyed by the revolution he effected and I am still more pleased to see him at the head of a fine, humane and even-handed government, which will encourage freedom of worship, enable agriculture, commerce and the arts to flourish, will establish internal peace, will punish the guilty but break the chains of those innocent victims who currently languish in prison cells and, above all, will solidly unite the French people so as to make them impregnable to attack from other countries. In view of all these blessings, who could refuse to utter from the bottom of his heart: Long live the Republic! Long live the government!

(c) My refusal to endorse the Constitution is based on the content of articles 39, 40, 41, 42 and 43 which, by investing so much authority in a single individual, could bring about the downfall of liberty in France, just as in the Roman era Julius Caesar and Claudius entombed the freedom of a once-renowned people.

(Examples of statements made by voters in the Var when passing judgement on the Constitution of the Year VIII in Nivôse (January 1800), cited in Poupé, *Le Département du Var*, 497–9. Translated.)

DOCUMENT XXI   Lucien Bonaparte explains the mission of the Prefects in 1800

Napoleon's younger brother, Lucien, played a vital role both in the coup and in its immediate aftermath. His contribution has seldom been recognized because Lucien soon fell out with his older brother and ended up as an exile in England. He was Minister of the Interior in 1800 and this address to the newly created prefects, who became key officials in the departments, neatly encapsulates the bureaucratic ethos of the nascent Bonapartist regime.

This post demands a wide range of duties, but it offers you great rewards in the future; you have been summoned to assist the government in its noble design to restore France to her ancient splendour, to revive in her all that is great and generous and to establish this magnificent edifice on the basis of liberty and equality . . . You will not be called upon to carry out the whims or passing desires of a fickle government, unstable in its operation and anxious about its future. Your first task is to destroy irrevocably, in your department, the influence of those events which for too long have dominated our minds. Do your utmost to bring hatred and passion to an end, to extinguish rancour, to blot out the painful memories of the past . . . In your public decisions and even in your private lives, be always the first magistrate of your department, never the man of the Revolution. Do not tolerate any public reference to the labels which still cling to the diverse political parties of the Revolution; merely consign them to that most deplorable chapter in the history of human folly . . . You will receive from the War Minister all the instructions necessary for the administrative responsibilities within his jurisdiction. I will simply limit myself to a reminder to apply yourself immediately to the conscription draft . . . I give special priority to the collection of taxes; their prompt payment is now a sacred duty. Agriculture, trade, the industries and professions must resume their honoured status. Respect and honour our farmers . . . Protect our trade whose freedom can never have any limit save for the public interest . . . Visit our manufactures; bestow your highest compliments on those distinguished citizens engaged in them . . . Encourage the new generations; fix your attention on public education, and the formation of Men, Citizens and Frenchmen.

(Cited in Lyons, *Napoleon Bonaparte*, 70.)

DOCUMENT XXII Decree limiting Parisian and Provincial Newspapers, 27 Nivôse VIII (17 January 1800)

Freedom of the press was a revolutionary ideal that had experienced a chequered history during the preceding decade. A born propagandist, Napoleon was convinced that newspapers should serve the interests of the government. A more draconian, and longer-lasting, form of press censorship was thus quickly established under the Consulate and its supervision was entrusted to the Minister of Police, Joseph Fouché.

The Consuls of the Republic, considering that some of the newspapers that are printed in the department of the Seine (Paris) are but instruments in the hands of the enemies of the Republic, and that the government is especially charged by the people to watch over its security, decrees the following:

1. During the entire course of the war, the minister of general police will only allow the printing, publication and distribution of the following newspapers . . . (thirteen titles follow), plus newspapers exclusively devoted to the sciences, arts, literature and commerce.

2. The minister of general police will report immediately on all the newspapers published in other departments.

3. The minister of general police will ensure that no newspaper is published simultaneously in the department of the Seine and any other department of the Republic.

4. The owners and editors of the newspapers retained after the present decree will present themselves to the minister of general police to provide proof of their virtue as French citizens, their place of residence and their personal signature, as well as a promise of loyalty to the Constitution.

5. All newspapers which include articles disrespectful towards the social order, to the sovereignty of the people and to the glory of the armies, or which publish attacks against governments friendly to, or allied with, the Republic, will be suppressed immediately, even if those articles are taken from the foreign press.

(P.-J.-B. Buchez and P.-C. Roux, *Histoire parlementaire de la Révolution française ou Journal des Assemblées nationales depuis 1789 jusqu'en 1815* (40 vols., Paris, 1838), vol. 38, 331–2.)

DOCUMENT XXIII   Law establishing Special Courts, 29 Pluviôse IX (7 February 1801)

In seeking to restore the rule of law in France, the Consulate had to overcome a wave of crime and resistance to government that the coup d'état had only worsened. Recourse to the sort of exceptional measures described in this extract could not be avoided. A wide variety of offenders were encompassed by this law of 1801, which created special courts to deliver summary justice in a manner reminiscent of the old regime.

I Formation and Organization
In those departments where the Government considers it necessary, a Special Court will be established for trying those accused of the crimes listed below.

These courts will comprise the president and two judges from the ordinary criminal court, plus three soldiers with the rank of at least captain, and two citizens possessing the qualities required of judges; the last category, as well as the military, will be chosen by the First Consul . . .

II Jurisdiction

These Special Courts will try crimes committed by vagrants and vagabonds and those condemned to corporal punishment . . .

It will also deal with vagrants and escaped criminals.

It will also deal with all those indicted for highway robbery, violence, assaults and other aggravated circumstances.

It will also assume competence over all persons charged with rural robberies and burglaries in rural dwellings and buildings where break-ins have occurred through walls, roofs, doors and windows, or when the crime has been conducted by at least two people carrying weapons.

It will also have jurisdiction over all persons . . . charged with premeditated murder.

It will equally take cognizance . . . of all persons charged with the crimes of arson, counterfeiting money, murders planned by armed groups; of threats, riots and assaults against purchasers of national property for reason of their purchase; of the crime of bribery of officials and of any misdoing practised outside the army, and by civilians, to corrupt or suborn soldiers, draftees and conscripts . . .

III Prosecution, investigation and judgement

All crimes assigned by title II to the Special Courts will be prosecuted officially and without delay . . .

Twenty-four hours after the arrival of the accused at the court house, he will be questioned . . .

After examination . . . the court will determine whether or not it has jurisdiction over the crime, without appeal . . . If it has jurisdiction, then it will proceed without delay to investigation and judgement . . .

The trial ended, the court will judge the matter as a final jurisdiction and without appeal. The crimes of robbery, violence, assault and burglary will be punished by death . . .

(J.-B. Duvergier (ed.), *Collection complète des lois, décrets, ordonnances, règlements, avis du Conseil d'État de 1788 à 1830* (30 vols., Paris, 1834–8), vol. 12, 366–70. Translated.)

DOCUMENT XXIV   The Concordat with the Papacy, 1801

Reconciliation was as important as repression in the restoration of stability under the Consulate. Bonaparte was well aware that the religious situation was a major cause of disaffection and he possessed few personal convictions in this regard that might stand in the way of a settlement. The Pope was equally anxious to strike a deal, which was sealed by the Concordat of 1801. The French Catholic Church was restored, but with none of its pre-revolutionary privileges as a religion of state or as a substantial property holder.

The First Consul of the French Republic and His Holiness the sovereign Pontiff, Pius VII, have named as their respective plenipotentiaries . . . who, after the exchange of their full respective powers and credentials, have settled on the following convention:

The government of the French Republic acknowledges that the Catholic, Apostolic and Roman religion is the religion of the great majority of French citizens. His Holiness equally realizes that this same religion has derived from, and at this moment expects, the greatest good and the greatest renown from the establishment of Catholic worship in France and from the personal profession of it made by the Consuls of the Republic. Consequently, after this mutual recognition, as much for the benefit of religion as for the maintenance of internal order, they have agreed to what follows:

1. The Catholic, Apostolic and Roman religion will be freely practised in France; its worship will be public and in conformity with those police regulations that the government judges necessary for public order.

2. The Holy See, in concert with the French government, will make a new division of French dioceses.

3. His Holiness will declare to the French bishops currently in post that, with firm confidence and for the benefit of peace and tranquillity, he expects them to make all manner of sacrifices, including that of their offices. After this exhortation, even if they should refuse to make this sacrifice, which is demanded for the good of the Church (though a refusal is not anticipated by His Holiness), he will nominate new bishops to the new dioceses in the following fashion:

4. The First Consul of the Republic will name incumbents for archbishoprics and bishoprics in the new division of dioceses, during the three months that follow the publication of His Holiness's Bull.

His Holiness will confer canonical authority, following the established forms used in France before the change of government [i.e. before the Revolution].

5. Nominations to bishoprics which fall vacant in future will also be made by the First Consul and canonical investiture will be granted by the Holy See in conformity with the preceding article.

6. Before assuming their functions, the bishops will swear directly, at the hands of the First Consul, the oath of loyalty which was in use before the change in government, expressed in the following terms:

> I swear and promise before God, on the Holy Gospel, to observe obedience and loyalty to the government established by the Constitution of the French Republic. I also promise to have no correspondence, nor to assist by counsel, nor to support any league, inside or outside France, which is contrary to public order. And if, in my diocese or elsewhere, I hear that anything prejudicial to the state is being plotted, I will make it known to the government.

7. Ecclesiastics of the second rank [i.e. parish priests] will swear the same oath at the hands of the civil authorities designated by the Government.

8. The following prayer will be recited at the end of divine worship in all Catholic churches in France: 'God save the Republic; God save the Consuls.'

9. Bishops will make new divisions of parishes in their dioceses, but these will only take effect after the government has approved them.

10. Bishops will nominate parish priests. Their choice may only include those men approved by the government.

11. The bishops may have a chapter in their cathedrals and a seminary for their diocese, without any obligation upon the government to endow either of them.

12. All metropolitan, cathedral, parochial and any unsold churches necessary for worship will be placed at the disposal of the bishops.

13. His Holiness, for the good of harmony and the happy re-establishment of the Catholic religion, declares that neither he nor his successors will in any way disturb the purchasers of alienated ecclesiastical property and that, as a consequence, the ownership of this property, together with the rights and revenues attached to them, will remain securely in their hands or with those whom they designate.

14. The government will guarantee an appropriate salary to bishops and priests whose parishes and dioceses are included in the new division.

15. The government will likewise take measures so that French Catholics may, if they wish, donate property to the Church.

16. His Holiness accords to the First Consul of the French Republic the rights enjoyed by the previous government [i.e. the old-regime monarchy].

17. It is agreed by the contracting parties that, in circumstances where one of the successors of the present First Consul is not a Catholic, the rights and prerogatives contained in the previous article, and the nomination of French bishops, will be regulated by a new convention.

Ratification will be made within the space of forty days.

Paris, 15 July 1801.

(Buchez and Roux, *Histoire parlementaire*, vol.38, 463–70. Translated.)

DOCUMENT XXV   Religious conflicts after the Concordat

The religious settlement brought Napoleon many advantages, but it should be stressed that it was by no means completely successful in resolving the conflicts of the revolutionary period. This report, which was probably prepared for the Minister of Police in 1803, suggests that tensions between anticlerical local authorities and politically suspect priests were a constant source of concern. Friction of this kind would continue to disrupt French society in the century that followed. The underlinings which appear in this extract were added by the evidently outraged author of the document.

I have already, on more than one occasion, drawn to your excellency's attention the conduct of a few turbulent priests, whose incorrigible obstinacy gives rise every day to fresh scenes of scandal.

Perhaps the most revolting incidents are those provoked by the refusal of church burial. These are also the most frequent.

In Fructidor the justice of the peace of the canton of Braine (Aisne) denounced the *curé* of that commune for refusing burial to Fouquet and Carguet deceased, because, he said, they had died without the benefit of sacrament, and that besides, the former was a married priest ...

Even more recently, Plochon, *curé* of Saint-Gervais (Vienne), refused to conduct a religious funeral for the mayor's assistant. He alleged that the deceased had never made his Easter confession and that he did not attend church services regularly.

The police commissioner of Nevers denounces several priests . . . accusing them of preaching disorder and anathematising purchasers of national properties . . .

The assistant mayor of Boisguillaume (Seine-Inférieure) denounces the priest Autin . . . for having refused the sacrament to two men on their deathbed, because they had been married by a constitutional priest. He has written to the Prefect and the Minister for Religion.

Fontelaye, curate of Rasnes (Orne), was denounced for recommending the King, the Queen and the Royal Family to his congregation from the pulpit at high mass . . . A prosecution was initiated. The facts were clearly proved, and were not even denied by Fontelaye, but he excused himself, claiming it was an accident which he calls a *lapsus linguae*. Several witnesses supported this allegation, the Prefect himself seemed to enjoy it, and ordered the matter to be dropped.

(Cited in Lyons, *Napoleon Bonaparte*, 90.)

DOCUMENT XXVI   Napoleon's Bulletin after the Battle of Marengo, June 1800

Military victory at Marengo, in Northern Italy, in June 1800 was a crucial element in the consolidation of the Consulate. For while Napoleon needed to establish peace within France, he also had to deal with the external enemies of the Republic. Defeat on the battlefield would be fatal for the regime, as Bonaparte's downfall in 1814/1815 demonstrated. Conversely, famous victories could be turned to tremendous propaganda effect, in military bulletins of the type reproduced here.

After the Battle of Montebello the army set out to pass through Scrivia. On 24 Prairial [13 June 1800], the advance guard commanded by General Gardanne encountered enemy forces, who were defending the approaches to the Bormida River and three bridges they held near Alessandria, and overcame them, taking two cannons and 100 prisoners in the process. The division led by General Chabran arrived at the same moment along the River Po, opposite Valenza, in order to prevent the enemy crossing. Thus Melas [the Austrian commander] found himself trapped between the Bormida and the Po. The only means of retreating from Genoa which remained open to him after the Battle of Montebello was cut off. The enemy appeared to have no idea what to do and was very uncertain of his movements.

On 25 Prairial [14 June] at dawn, the enemy attempted to cross the Bormida at the three bridges and, determined to get through, emerged in force, to take our advance guard by surprise; thus began, in an extremely spirited fashion, the famous battle of Marengo, which would finally decide the fate of Italy and the Austrian army. Four times during the battle we were forced to retreat and four times we advanced. At different points in the battle more than sixty pieces of artillery changed hands. More than twelve cavalry charges took place, with varying degrees of success.

At 3 p.m., 10,000 cavalrymen overran our right flank on the superb plain of San Giuliano. They were supported by a line of cavalry and plenty of artillery. But the grenadiers of the consular guard formed a granite-like redoubt in the middle of this immense plain and nothing could shift them. Cavalry, infantry and artillery were all thrown against this battalion, but in vain; there one could truly observe what a handful of courageous men could achieve. As a result of this stubborn resistance the enemy's left flank was contained and our right wing was sustained, until General Monnier arrived, having seized the village of Castel Ceriolo at bayonet-point. The enemy made a rapid thrust along our left flank, which had already been unsettled, and this manœuvre precipitated our retreat. The enemy now advanced all along the line, raking it with a hail of fire from over 100 cannons. The roads were full of men in retreat, the wounded and much debris; the battle appeared to be lost . . .

The presence of the First Consul revived the morale of the troops. 'My boys', he said to them, 'remember that it is my custom to sleep on the field of battle.' To cries of 'Long live the Republic!' and 'Long live the First Consul!' Desaix arrived at the gallop and charged through the centre. In a flash the enemy was vanquished. General Kellermann who, with his brigade of heavy cavalry had protected our retreating left flank all day, carried out a timely charge with such force that 6,000 Austrian grenadiers and General Zach, chief of staff, were taken prisoner, while several enemy generals were killed.

The entire French army followed up this attack. The enemy's right flank was cut off; confusion and terror swept through its ranks. The

Austrian cavalry was brought to the centre to protect the retreat, but General Bessières, at the head of a bunch of dare-devils and grenadiers from the consular guard, led a charge with as much briskness as valour and broke the line of enemy cavalry; it brought the complete rout of the enemy army. We took fifteen standards, forty cannons and 6,000–8,000 prisoners. More than 6,000 of the enemy were left dead on the battlefield.

The ninth light infantry brigade deserved its title 'incomparable'. The heavy cavalry and the eighth dragoons covered themselves in glory too. Our losses were considerable, however; we had 600 men killed, 1,500 wounded and 900 taken prisoner. Generals Champeaux, Mainoni and Boudet were wounded. General Berthier had his uniform riddled with bullets; several of his aides lost their horses. But one loss, as keenly felt by the army, as it will be by the entire Republic, took the joy from our hearts. Desaix was hit at the start of the charge he led and died instantly. He only had time to say to young Lebrun, who was with him, 'Go and tell the First Consul that I die regretting that I have not done enough to survive in the memory of future generations.'

In the course of his life, General Desaix had four horses killed under him and was severely wounded three times. He had only rejoined our headquarters just three days earlier; he was thirsting for battle and two or three times the previous day he had said to his aides: 'It has been a long time since I fought in Europe. I am no longer used to bullets, I am sure something will happen to me.' In the midst of intense fire, when someone came to announce Desaix's death to the First Consul, he uttered only the words: 'Why shouldn't I weep?' Desaix's corpse has been sent to Milan for embalming.

(Napoleon, *Correspondance*, vol.6, 453–6. Translated.)

DOCUMENT XXVII   The Life Consulate, 1802

The offer of the Consulate for life was the product of a political manœuvre led by Napoleon's closest political allies in the Senate. In this extract, Bonaparte responds to the invitation in a typically meretricious fashion, linking his destiny to that of the French people, who overwhelmingly endorsed this enhancement of his dictatorship in the accompanying referendum.

Message of Napoleon to the Senate accepting the Life Consulate, 15
Thermidor X (3 August 1802)

Senators, the life of a citizen belongs to his *patrie*. The French people
wish that mine be entirely devoted to it. I obey its will. In giving me a
new pledge, a permanent pledge of its confidence, it imposes upon
me the duty of consolidating its system of laws on well-founded
institutions. By my efforts and with your co-operation, Citizen
Senators, by the assistance of all the authorities, with the confidence
and will of this immense people, the liberty, equality and prosperity
of France will be sheltered from the caprice of fate and the
uncertainty of the future. The best of peoples will be the happiest of
peoples, as it deserves to be, and its bliss will contribute to that of all
Europe.

   Content to have been called, by order of Him from whom
everything comes, to re-establish justice, order and equality on earth,
I will hear my last hour strike without regret and without anxiety as
far as the opinion of posterity is concerned. Senators, receive my
thanks for taking so solemn a step. The Senate desired what the
French people wished and, as a result, it is more closely associated
with all that remains to be done for the happiness of the *patrie* . . .

(Napoleon, *Correspondance*, vol.7, 702. Translated.)

DOCUMENT XXVIII   The First Empire, 1804

The creation of the First Empire in 1804 represented the logical conclusion
to Napoleon's seizure of power in Brumaire (November 1799), quite
literally crowning the consolidation of his supreme authority in France.
This final stage in his personal elevation was not planned from the outset;
like so much of his career, it was brilliantly improvised as circumstances
permitted. Its anti-feminism in excluding women from the imperial dignity
stands out today, though a Bonapartist dynasty was not to be established.
Napoleon did eventually sire a male heir from his second marriage, but his
son never ruled because the Empire disappeared with the downfall of its
architect in 1814.

Senatus Consultum establishing the imperial Constitution, 7 Prairial XII
(18 May 1804)

I

The government of the Republic is entrusted to an emperor, who takes the title 'Emperor of the French'. Justice is dispensed, in the name of the emperor, by the officials he appoints. Napoleon Bonaparte, currently First Consul of the Republic, has become Emperor of the French.

II

The imperial dignity is hereditary in the direct, natural, legitimate lineage of Napoleon Bonaparte, from male to male, by order of primogeniture, to the perpetual exclusion of women and their lineage.

(Godechot, *Les Constitutions de la France*, 185. Translated.)

Glossary

A note on the revolutionary calendar

One of the difficulties confronting students of the Directory and the Consulate is presented by the republican calendar, which was in official use from the autumn of 1793 until the end of 1805. The foundation of the First French Republic on 22 September 1792, had already become the first day of Year I, though the months were not reorganized for another year, at the outset of the Year II. The twelve revolutionary months, of thirty days each, were named according to the time of year: hence Vendémiaire (September–October), the time of the grape harvest, or Brumaire (October–November), the time of fog. Unfortunately the new months do not coincide with the old and, despite the wish of members of the National Convention to introduce regularity with twelve equal months, nature was not so easily accommodated. To arrive at a total of 365 days in the year, not to mention making allowance for leap years, a variable number of additional days had to be added to the end of each republican year. The precise equivalent between the republican and Christian calendars thus varies slightly from year to year, but the approximate concordance is as follows:

Vendémiaire	late September to late October
Brumaire	late October to late November
Frimaire	late November to late December
Nivôse	late December to late January
Pluviôse	late January to late February
Ventôse	late February to late March
Germinal	late March to late April
Floréal	late April to late May
Prairial	late May to late June
Messidor	late June to late July
Thermidor	late July to late August
Fructidor	late August to late September

For a good introduction to the significance of the revolutionary calendar, see Mona Ozouf, 'Revolutionary calendar', in François Furet and Mona Ozouf (eds.), *A Critical Dictionary of the French Revolution*, translated by Arthur Goldhammer (Belknap Press, Cambridge, Mass., 1989), 538–47.

ASSIGNATS. Paper money introduced in 1790, secured on the basis of future receipts from the sale of national lands (see below). In fact, the cash-strapped revolutionaries turned them into a paper currency that rapidly lost value and generated hyper-inflation. The *assignats* were abolished in 1796 and the *mandats territoriaux*, the paper money that replaced them, were totally discredited within twelve months. It was then decided to return to hard cash.

BIENS NATIONAUX. Property confiscated during the Revolution, at first from the Church, then later from *émigrés*, suspects and persons condemned for crimes against the Revolution, which was taken into national or state ownership for subsequent sale to private purchasers.

BRUMAIRIANS. The coalition of moderate politicians, leading officials and military personnel who overthrew the Directory on 18–19 Brumaire VIII.

CHOUANS. Peasant rebels in the west of France, in Brittany and Normandy, who waged guerrilla warfare against the Republic from the mid-1790s down to the Consulate. Their name apparently originated from the call of the screech-owl that was used as a signal among them.

COMMISSAIRES DU DIRECTOIRE EXÉCUTIF. Officials, mostly former revolutionary administrators, who were appointed by the Directory to keep an eye on all locally elected administrations and courts, according to the 1795 Constitution. The *commissaires* have been seen as forerunners of the Napoleonic prefects, whose powers were far more extensive.

CONSUL. A term of Roman derivation, not to be confused with ambassadors, but referring to a member of the executive of the Republic after Brumaire. Hence the name of the regime from the end of 1799 until 1804: the Consulate.

CONVENTIONNEL. A member of the National Convention, the parliamentary body first elected in August 1792, which only dissolved three years later in 1795. Even then, thanks to the 'law of the two-thirds', many *conventionnels* remained in the Legislature during the years of the Directory that followed.

COUP D'ÉTAT. This term was little used in the Revolution, when 'revolution' or *journée* (see below) were usually employed to denote a sudden transformation of the political scene. Its application to the events of Fructidor V (1797) and Brumaire VIII (1799) seems reasonable, but it is more debatable as a description of the decree of the two-thirds (1795), or the events of Floréal VI (1798) and Prairial VII (1799).

DÉPARTEMENTS. The administrative units created by the Revolution in 1790, originally led by elected bodies, were placed under a prefect by Napoleon, who is often wrongly credited with creating them. There were originally eighty-three departments but, as the Republic expanded territorially, new ones were added, until there were 103 when Bonaparte came to power. (See map 2 on p. xii).

ÉMIGRÉS. Disaffected nobles began leaving revolutionary France as early as 1789, but the trickle soon turned into a flood, and priests and ordinary persons emigrated in their turn. These *émigrés*, of whom there were some 150,000, had been subject to harsh penalities which entailed loss of property and in some cases loss of life. They posed a significant problem which Bonaparte was eventually to resolve with a more conciliatory approach.

FLORÉAL. Revolutionary month of April–May, which earned notoriety after the annulment of election results of the Year VI (1798). Voters had returned many left-wing deputies, who were unwelcome to the Directory and were consequently rejected, or '*floréalisé*'.

FRUCTIDOR. The revolutionary month of September–October became notorious after the Directory purged right-wing opponents from the Legislature on 18 Fructidor V (4 September 1797). Victims in parliament and in the local administration were '*fructidorisé*', or removed from office and prosecuted, sometimes put to death, in the crack-down that followed.

JACOBINS. Name given to radical revolutionaries, who met in the Jacobin (or Dominican) monastery in Paris and led a nation-wide network of clubs that dominated France in 1793. They revived under the Directory as left-wing opponents of the liberal Republic, when they are often referred to as 'neo-Jacobins', though this was not a term used at the time.

NOTABLES. Those whose names appeared on the Napoleonic electoral lists after 1801, though historians employ the term for the ruling classes (an amalgam of nobles and wealthy bourgeois) who emerged as an 'aristocracy of wealth' following the abolition of noble privilege in the Revolution.

PATRIE. Literally fatherland, or France.

PLEBISCITE. Another Roman term, whose modern equivalent is the referendum – though neither word was actually used for these 'votes on the Constitution' – which took place in 1793 and 1795 during the Revolution and then under Bonaparte in the Years VIII (1800), X (1802) and XII (1804), and finally in 1815.

PLUS IMPOSÉS. The highest taxpayers in each department, from whose ranks the members of the departmental electoral colleges were drawn after 1802.

REFRACTORY PRIESTS. Those Roman Catholic clergy who refused to swear an oath of allegiance to the Revolution, following the imposition of changes in the Church which came with the Civil Constitution of the Clergy in 1790. Another three oaths were imposed on the clergy after 1791 and refractories (as opposed to 'constitutional', or 'juring priests' who did swear) were liable to severe penalties. Bonaparte resolved the problem with the Concordat introduced in 1802.

SANS-CULOTTES. Literally 'without breeches', a reference to the militant working men of revolutionary Paris, mostly craftsmen and artisans, who wore long trousers rather than the knee-breeches and silk stockings affected by the middle and upper classes.

SENATUS CONSULTUM. Procedure first adopted in 1801, which allowed the Senate (employing its power to amend the Constitution) to issue constitutional changes and other laws that Bonaparte wished to introduce, bypassing the Legislature; effectively rule by decree. Plural *senatus consulta*.

SOLS. The pre-revolutionary monetary system in France was remarkably similar to the old British shillings and pounds. That is to say that twenty *sols* made one *livre*. The Revolution introduced a decimal system of *centimes* and *francs*, though it took a long time to come into full use.

THERMIDORIANS. The coalition of supporters of the Terror (such as Barras and Fouché), friends of Danton, and various moderates who brought down Robespierre on 9 Thermidor of the Year II (27 July 1794) and who dominated the last phase of the National Convention until it finally separated in September 1795.

VENDÉE. Location of a violent peasant insurrection against the Republic which began in 1793 and proved a running sore until the Consulate; named after the western department in which it erupted, though it affected neighbouring departments too (see map 2 on p. xii).

Further Reading

(a) Background reading on the Revolutionary and Napoleonic periods

Jeremy D. Popkin, *A Short History of the French Revolution* (Englewood-Cliffs, Prentice-Hall, 1995). The best, brief introduction to the Revolution currently available; encompasses the Napoleonic era as well as the revolutionary decade.

Willam Doyle, *The Oxford History of the French Revolution* (Oxford, Oxford University Press, 1989). The standard history of the Revolution, a magisterial survey which includes the Directory and ends with a consideration of the Consulate.

Donald M. G. Sutherland, *Revolution and Counter-Revolution in France, 1789–1815* (London, Fontana, 1985). A superb overview, which contains a wealth of fascinating material on the provinces. Not perhaps for the novice, but extremely rewarding for the more advanced student.

Michael J. Sydenham, *The First French Republic, 1792–1804* (London, Batsford, 1974). Provides an excellent political narrative of the period after the fall of Robespierre and embraces the establishment of the Napoleonic regime as well as the downfall of the Directory.

François Furet, *The French Revolution, 1770–1814,* translated by Antonia Nevill (Cambridge, Polity Press, 1996). A somewhat idiosyncratic but always stimulating view of the period, though not for beginners.

Alfred Cobban, *A History of Modern France,* vol. 1: *1715–1789;* vol.2: *1799–1871* (Harmondsworth, Penguin, first ed. 1957 and 1961). This extremely readable survey is still available, but badly dated. The author admits that it is difficult to say much about the Directory; only fifteen pages, out of 100 on the revolutionary decade, are devoted to it in vol.1; there is no more than a brief description of the *coup d'état* of Brumaire, the aftermath of which is dealt with in vol.2.

Albert Soboul, *The French Revolution 1787-1799*, 2 vols., translated by Alan Forrest and Colin Jones (London, New Left Books, 1974). A classic Marxist interpretation of the Revolution, which concludes with Bonaparte's advent to power, represented as a dictatorship of the bourgeoisie.

(b) Biographies of Napoleon

Biographies of Napoleon are legion; he is said to have attracted more scholarly attention than any other individual save Jesus Christ. Many of them concentrate upon his private life, notably his relationship with Josephine. Most of these books are based on second-hand accounts and should be avoided. Try the following instead:

Maurice Hutt, *Napoleon* (Oxford, Oxford University Press, 1965), a slim volume and an excellent starting-point; Felix Markham, *Napoleon* (London, 1963), a good 'man and his times' approach; Georges Lefebvre, *Napoleon*, translated by Henry Stockhold and J.E. Anderson (2 vols., London, Routledge & Kegan Paul, 1969), the first volume most directly relevant to the rise of Napoleon; a classic work from a leading authority on the Revolution, but the translation (as so often when made by a non-historian) is sometimes faulty; Jean Tulard, *Napoleon or the Myth of the Saviour*, translated by Teresa Waugh (London, Methuen, 1984), none too well rendered into English, but this is the standard critical biography from the *doyen* of French historians on Bonaparte; Martyn Lyons, *Napoleon Bonaparte and the Legacy of the French Revolution* (Basingstoke, Macmillan, 1994), an extremely accessible survey of the Napoleonic period, which opens with chapters on Napoleon's rise to power and the establishment of his regime, a trifle harsh on the Directory, but excellent on the social basis of Bonapartism; Geoffrey Ellis, *Napoleon* (Longman Profiles in Power, London, 1996), by no means a straightforward biography; as the series title suggests, this focuses upon the sinews of power in the Napoleonic regime, expanding the same author's earlier, and shorter, study, *The Napoleonic Empire* (Macmillan Studies in European History, Basingstoke, 1991). Finally, there is a good account of Brumaire in an older study by John Holland Rose, *The Life of Napoleon I* (London, G. Bell and Sons, 1913).

(c) Historiography

Pieter Geyl, *Napoleon For and Against* (Harmondsworth, Penguin, 1965). First published fifty years ago, this is a classic of the genre which reviews French approaches to Bonaparte, from the nineteenth century to the Second World War.

John Dunne, 'Napoleon For and Against . . . and Beyond', *History Review*, 27 (1997), 17–21. A good update.

Works referred to in the account of the historical debate on the rise of Napoleon, which have been translated into English, include: G. de Staël, *Considerations on the Principal Events of the French Revolution* (London, G. Charpentier, 1818); Pierre Lanfrey, *The History of Napoleon the First* (4 vols., Oxford, Macmillan, 1871–9); and Alphonse Aulard, *The French Revolution: A Political History, 1789– 1804* (4 vols., London, T. Fisher Unwin, 1910).

(d) The Directory

Martyn Lyons, *France under the Directory* (Cambridge, Cambridge University Press, 1975). A new history of the Directory is badly needed, especially in view of recent work which should permit a more nuanced assessment. Lyons's survey remains the best available; it has worn well. There are two overviews translated from French: Georges Lefebvre, *The Directory*, translated by Robert Baldick (London, Routledge, 1965), only a shadow of Lefebvre's more extensive survey of these years, which is available only in French; Denis Woronoff, *The Thermidorian Regime and the Directory*, translated by Julian Jackson (Cambridge, Cambridge University Press, 1984). This solid survey of the period from the fall of Robespierre was first published in France ten years earlier.

There are two stimulating essays which discuss the general nature and achievements of the Directory: Albert Goodwin, 'The French Executive Directory – a re-evaluation', *History*, 22 (1937), and Clive H. Church, 'In Search of the Directory', in John F. Bosher (ed.), *French Government and Society, 1500–1850: Essays in Memory of Alfred Cobban* (London, Athlone Press, 1973), 261–94.

Aspects of the period are covered in the following, which often throw a good deal of light on the period after Bonaparte came to power:

Military matters have naturally bulked large. T. C. W. Blanning, *The French Revolutionary Wars, 1787–1802* (London, Edward Arnold, 1996), provides the essential background to the rise of Napoleon as a general, in this author's usual, invigorating manner. On the army there are: Alan Forrest, *The Soldiers of the French Revolution* (Durham, NC and London, Duke University Press, 1990) and the same author's *Conscripts and Deserters: The Army and French Society during the Revolution and Empire* (Oxford, Oxford University Press, 1989), and Jean-Paul Bertaud, *The Army of the French Revolution*, translated by Robert Palmer (Princeton, Princeton University Press, 1988). Howard G. Brown has linked the military to administrative aspects of the period in *War, Revolution and the Bureaucratic State: Politics and Army Administration in France, 1791–1799* (Oxford, Clarendon Press, 1995), querying Clive H. Church, *Revolution and Red Tape: The French Ministerial Bureaucracy 1770–1850* (Oxford, Clarendon Press, 1981) in the process.

Problems of law and order have also received attention, notably from students of Richard Cobb and Colin Lucas. Cobb's own contributions include: *The Police and the People: French Popular Protest, 1789–1820* (Oxford, Oxford University Press, 1970), *Reactions to the French Revolution* (Oxford, Oxford University Press, 1972) and *Paris and its Provinces* (Oxford, Oxford University Press, 1975). Lucas has written two influential articles: 'The First Directory and the rule of law', *French Historical Studies*, 10 (1977), 231–60, and 'The rules of the game of politics under the Directory', *French Historical Studies*, 16 (1989), 345–71. Gwynne Lewis and Colin Lucas have edited *Beyond the Terror: Essays in French Regional and Social History, 1794–1815* (Cambridge, Cambridge University Press, 1983), which contains some excellent essays on crime and violence, as well as pieces on welfare, the Church and the countryside.

There are some interesting articles on law ond order too: Charles Doyle, 'Internal counter-revolution: the judicial reaction in southern France, 1794–1800', *Renaissance and Modern Studies*, 33 (1989), 106–24; Jonathan D. Devlin, 'The army and the politics of military command: the army of the interior in south-east France', *French History*, 4 (1990), 199–223; and Howard G. Brown, 'From organic society to security state: the war on brigandage in France, 1797–1802', *Journal of Modern History*, 69 (1997), 661–95.

Political life has received considerable attention. Isser Woloch, *The*

New Regime: Transformations of the French Civic Order, 1789–1820s (NewYork and London, W. W. Norton, 1994), shows just how much, and equally how little, change was achieved, in a rare work which straddles the revolutionary and Napoleonic decades and gives the Directory its due. The press has been studied a good deal of late, and Jeremy D. Popkin, *Revolutionary News: The Press in France, 1789–1799* (Durham, NC, and London, Duke University Press, 1990), offers a good introduction. See the same author's more specific study: *The Right-Wing Press in France, 1792–1800* (Chapel Hill, University of North Carolina Press, 1980). Malcolm Crook, *Elections in the French Revolution: An Apprenticeship in Democracy, 1789–1799* (Cambridge, Cambridge University Press, 1996), puts elections into perspective, while Isser Woloch, *Jacobin Legacy: the Democratic Movement under the Directory* (Princeton, Princeton University Press, 1970), rescues the democratic left from historical oblivion under the Directory, and R. B. Rose, *Gracchus Babeuf: The First Revolutionary Communist* (London, Edward Arnold, 1978), provides a good study of the Communist forerunner.

For the counter-revolution, see Jacques Godechot's classic survey, *The Counter-Revolution: Doctrine and Action, 1789–1815*, translated by Salvator Attanasio (London, Routledge and Kegan Paul, 1972), and James Roberts's brief overview, *The Counter-Revolution in France 1787–1830* (Basingstoke, Macmillan, 1990). More detailed studies include: W. R. Fryer, *Republic or Restoration in France, 1794–1797: D'André and the Politics of French Royalism* (Manchester, Manchester University Press, 1965); Harvey Mitchell, *The Underground War against Revolutionary France: The Missions of William Wickham 1794–1800* (Oxford, Oxford University Press, 1965); and Donald Sutherland, *The Chouans: The Social Origins of Popular Counter-Revolution in Upper Brittany, 1770–1796* (Oxford, Oxford University Press, 1982).

For religious aspects, consult the later chapters of John McManners, *The French Revolution and the Church* (SPCK, London, 1969), a splendidly readable survey, which remains serviceable after nearly thirty years.

Aside from Richard Cobb, *Death in Paris, 1795-1801* (Oxford, Oxford University Press, 1978), and sections in Alan Forrest, *The French Revolution and the Poor* (Oxford, Blackwell, 1981), there is little in English on social and economic aspects of the Directory. Some information in this regard may be gleaned from studies of the provinces during this period. They include the following: Jeffry Kaplow, *Elbeuf during the Revolutionary Period: History and Social Structure* (Baltimore, Johns Hopkins University Press, 1964); Gwynne Lewis, *The Second Vendée: The Continuity of Counter-Revolution in the Department of the Gard, 1789–1815* (Oxford, Oxford University Press, 1978); Malcolm Crook, *Toulon in War and Revolution: From the Ancien Régime to the Restoration, 1750–1820* (Manchester, Manchester University Press, 1991); and Alan Forrest, *The Revolution in Provincial France: Aquitaine, 1789–1799* (Oxford, Oxford University Press, 1996).

(e) Brumaire

J. Goodspeed, *Bayonets at Saint-Cloud* (London, Rupert Hart-Davis, 1965); in the absence of a translation of Vandal's great work, *L'Avènement de Bonaparte*, this is the best account of the *coup* in English. Lynn Hunt, David Lansky and Paul Hanson explore the parliamentary personnel involved in the events of Brumaire in an important article entitled: 'The road to Brumaire: the failure of the liberal Republic in France, 1795–1799', *Journal of Modern History*, 51 (1979), 734–59.

Two books in French should also be mentioned: the brief study by Jean-Paul Bertaud, *Bonaparte prend le pouvoir* (Brussels, Editions Complexes, 1987), and the more substantial survey by Thierry Lentz, *Le 18-Brumaire. Les coups d'état de Napoléon Bonaparte* (Paris, Jean Picollec, 1997).

(f) Consulate to Empire

There is no single book in English on the Consulate. It is a period that has received scant attention, even in France, so what follows is confined to certain aspects of the period.

Frank Kafker and James Laux (eds.) *Napoleon and his Times* (Malabar, Fla., Robert E. Krieger, 1989), contains selections of untranslated work in French, most notably from Vandal's classic *L'Avènement de Bonaparte* and Claude Langlois's *exposé* of the fraudulent plebiscite of the Year VIII. Irene Collins has written *Napoleon: First Consul and Emperor of the French*, New Appreciations in History (London, Historical Association, revised ed., 1993), and

Napoleon and his Parliaments, 1800–1815 (London, Edward Arnold, 1979). Robert B. Holtman, *The Napoleonic Revolution* (Baton Rouge and London, Louisiana State University Press, 1967), focuses on the Consulate, as do the early chapters of Geoffrey Ellis, *The Napoleonic Empire* (London, Macmillan, 1991). Louis Bergeron, *France under Napoleon*, translated by Robert Palmer (Princeton, Princeton University Press, 1981), is especially useful on economic and social aspects of the Napoleonic era, in this general survey originally published in 1972. There are two studies of the Concordat: E. E. Y. Hales, *Napoleon and the Pope: The Story of Napoleon and Pius VII* (London, Eyre & Spottiswoode, 1962) and H. H. Walsh, *The Concordat of 1801: A Study of the Problem of Nationalism in the Relations of Church and State* (New York, Columbia University Press, 1933). E. A. Whitcomb, 'Napoleonic prefects', *American Historical Review*, 79 (1974), 1089– 1118, offers an interesting study of the key administrative personnel in the provinces, while M. J. Sydenham explores opponents of the Consulate and the government's draconian response in 'The crime of 3 Nivôse (24 December 1800)', in J. F. Bosher (ed.), *French Government and Society, 1500–1850: Essays in Memory of Alfred Cobban* (London, Athlone Press, 1973), 295–320. Michael Broers, *Europe under Napoleon 1799–1815* (London, Arnold, 1996), provides an excellent survey of the wider context.

(g) Documentation and Works of Reference

Eric A. Arnold Jr. (ed. and trans.), *A Documentary Survey of Napoleonic France* (Lanham, Md. and London, University Press of America, 1994), and *A Supplement* which appeared in 1996 with the same publisher, offer the only comprehensive collection of documents in English, albeit one restricted to official texts.

Maurice Hutt (ed.), *Napoleon*, Great Lives Observed (Englewood Cliffs, Prentice-Hall, 1972) contains material from Napoleon, as well as contemporary and historical opinion, and some useful commentary from the editor. J. C. Herold (ed.), *The Mind of Napoleon* (New York, Columbia University Press, 1955), affords insight into the mind of the man, as does John Eldred Howard (ed.), *Letters and Documents of Napoleon, 1769-1802* (London, Cresset Press, 1961).

There are two relevant dictionaries from an English publisher:

Colin Jones, *The Longman Companion to the French Revolution* (Harlow, Longman, 1988), which is the best work of reference on the Revolution; masses of fascinating information are presented in an extremely accessible fashion; Clive Emsley, *The Longman Companion to Napoleonic Europe* (Harlow, Longman, 1993), covers Europe as a whole and is inevitably brief where France is concerned. Two from the USA are: Samuel F. Scott and Barry Rothaus (eds.), *Historical Dictionary of the French Revolution, 1789–1799* (2 vols., Westport CT and London, Greenwood Press, 1985); and Owen Connelly (ed.), *Historical Dictionary of Napoleonic France, 1799–1815* (Westport and London, Greenwood Press, 1985).

François Furet and Mona Ozouf (eds.), *A Critical Dictionary of the French Revolution*, translated by Arthur Goldhammer (Cambridge, Mass., and London, Belknap Press, 1989), have produced a series of stimulating, reflective essays rather than an all-embracing dictionary, as the title suggests. See especially the essays by Furet on Napoleon and by Denis Richet on *coups d'état*.

Index